to Mormons,
with LOVE

(a little something from the new girl in Utah)

chrisy ross

D1636823

American Fork
Arts Council Press

AMERICAN FORK, UTAH

AMERICAN FORK ARTS COUNCIL

Cover art: Darrell Driver
Cover design: Delphine Keim-Campbell
Chapter illustrations: Darrell Driver
Map: Taylor Hinton
Family and author photos: Justin Hackworth
Page layout: Mark Calkins
Layout advisor: Delphine Keim-Campbell

ISBN 978-1-60574-001-0

For Georgeanna E Fisher and Mary Jane Hautem, my grandmothers.

I still feel you.

CONTENTS

Acknowledgments

Many people believed this project had a place in space, many people have encouraged and supported my writing over the years; have generally believed in me. But one man's calm and confident answer when I asked, "Do you think this is publishable?" is literally the sole reason I saw this book through to completion. Caleb Warnock said yes and guided me every step of the way. Buckets of gratitude to you, Caleb.

To early readers who provided critiques and candid feedback, your fingerprints are on these pages. Thank you, Kailee Savage, Robin Roberts, Melissa Richardson, Matt Evans, Christopher Stallings, Marnie Stallings, Kristin Stockham, Mrs. H., Steph Lineback, and all of my fellow students who attend Wednesday night writing class.

Special thanks go to friends who have provided *miscellaneous* assistance and all around good juju. Thank you, Taylor Hinton, Carene Battaglia, Christy Casimiro, Jill Williamson, and Veronica Deschambault.

And two friends, who I'm confident my husband joins me in thanking because they fill my leaky wells, Amy DesRosier and Todd Mitchell.

Darrell Driver created the beautiful cover art specifically for the book. I simply love it. Gracias, Darrell. Then Delphine Keim-Campbell defied time constraints and produced a stunning cover design. I can't thank you enough, Del—for the cover, layout design, discovering my use of the word "saddle" when I meant "sidle", and for being my friend.

Without Mark and Kathy Calkins, this book would not exist... for many reasons. From providing the opportunity for our family to move to Utah, to your gracious help getting the book in a publishable format, Chris and I extend our deepest gratitude.

I feel indebted to the city of American Fork, and the American Fork Arts Council, led by Lori England, for supporting the arts in full. The commitment to local writers through the creation of classes, conferences, and a press has benefited amateur and professional writers from across the state and beyond. Everyone involved deserves a standing ovation. I'm humbled by the dedication of those who give their time, financial resources, and talent. I stand in a line of many who say thank you.

Our three sons have stretched in many ways to support the writing and publishing of this book. Parke, Duke and Redmond, I couldn't be more proud to be your mother. Thank you for taking on a little more and exercising patience. You're all three an example to me. My love for you is truly boundless.

Chris, my husband, has read every word I've ever written and rewritten. Multiple times. He doesn't love everything I write, but he loves me. Thank you for helping me cultivate the moments to work and for maintaining a healthy perspective when I've lost mine. Our boys are your sons. Lucky me.

Introduction

Nonmembers Anonymous

Hi. My name is Chris. I live in Mayberry, Utah County, Utah, and I'm not a member of the Mormon Church. I'm happy living here. They say admission is the first step.

○●○

My husband and I have lived in our small Mormon community since November 2002. We have three sons, a dog, a bird, and a fish. After a job-related move brought us to Utah, we purchased a home in an area that was less religiously diverse than we had anticipated. Everyone was Mormon. Everyone.

I thought I knew more than the average non-Mormon about the Faith, but I was wrong. I didn't know what a "ward" was, "member" made me think of Costco, and "LDS" sounded like the drug I was afraid to try in college.

I assumed all Mormon mothers stayed home with their well mannered, attractive children and pondered what healthy meal they would serve for dinner. I quickly learned the only consistently true words in that last sentence are "attractive children." I'm still looking for the neighborhood ugly child.

Since our arrival in Utah County, I've learned that there is no secret handshake (or is there?), there is not a CIA-type file on our family at the church, members do not receive points on a literal scoreboard for attempts to convert us, and there is diversity within Mormonism. It's true that Mormons don't drink alcohol, coffee or tea (cough), and they never use foul language (double cough).

We gradually assimilated into the community, but only after working through subtle culture shock, which included irritation at all things new and different. I counted steeples, rolled my eyes at Costco's food storage items, and shamelessly stared at the arms and thighs of strangers, searching for garment lines. All of them—steeples, giant cans of peaches, and garments—were reminders of the pervasive religion of which I was not a part. Paranoia that I was only a missionary opportunity made me suspicious of every person's attempt at friendship.

The culture shock, paranoia, and loneliness I experienced morphed into an understanding and appreciation of the Utah County culture, my community and home. The stories, experiences and perspective in this book are mine only and are based on cultural, not doctrinal, observations. My humble research has revealed that the Church does not support, endorse or encourage intolerance of others' beliefs, shunning, or naughty behavior in general.

What You Need To Know

1. I am not LDS.

2. My intention is not to debate, dissuade, persuade or change any person's faith or belief. Who needs a poke in the eye?

3. I have read the *Book of Mormon* (twice-ish) and sections of the *Doctrine and Covenants*.

4. I strive not to be a basher. Of anything.

5. I love living where I do and am thankful for my Mormon peeps. Although culturally not for everyone (including some LDS families), life in a small, Utah County town has been—dare I say—a blessing.

We're frequently asked, "How did you end up *here?*" and "What's it *really* like living here for you guys?" Read along and I'll tell you.

PART I

In The Beginning

Mayberry By Accident

In the fall of 2002, my husband, also named Chris, accepted a job in Provo, Utah, that required us to relocate with our two young sons from Castle Rock, Colorado. I had never been to Utah and was excited to visit the state on our house-hunting trip. Chris shared how beautiful the Salt Lake City and Provo areas were. He said, "Utah's more like Colorado than Colorado is."

The press from the 2002 Winter Olympics, hosted in Salt Lake City, had demystified some of the misconceptions associated with the Mormon Church and answered many questions. I was confident that not only would we be able to purchase alcohol and coffee in Utah, but we would also find a nice neighborhood with a smattering of diversity.

House Hunting

As we walked through homes, it was evident which ones were LDS households and which ones were not. Something I became acutely aware of. I tried to pretend I didn't notice the large portraits of Jesus Christ or other faith-related artwork, but I was fascinated and slightly distracted. I scanned kitchen countertops for coffee makers, searched stovetops for teapots, and looked for any evidence of an imbiber. If I didn't see LDS effects, I looked for other faith identifiers: a cross, a Star of David, a Jesus fish (still not sure what that means), a Buddha statue or a peace sign. I was silently tabulating.

I'd heard about Mormon food storage in the early 80s. I envisioned a bomb shelter—like the kind Howard Cunningham wanted to purchase on a 1974 episode of the sitcom "Happy Days"—full of Chef Boyardee products in case Russians attacked. I'd also heard that Mormons didn't drink Pepsi or Coke, so I left my assumptions in the past.

When the Realtor flipped the light switch on in the first basement storage area, it took me a few moments to process all of the diapers, baby formula, powdered food and canned goods. Large cans. She gestured toward the sturdy shelves and said, "This is your storage area." She admired the space and added, "Very nice." We followed her as she walked toward another door at the end of the small room. "And here's the under-porch storage," she said.

Under-porch storage? The concept was slightly titillating. The Realtor opened the door and I saw large barrels stacked on top of one another. I couldn't imagine what they contained. My mind raced from gunpowder to body parts to chemicals.

"What's all this?" I asked.

"Probably wheat, and these are water," she answered.

We were introduced to basement "dry" and "cold" storage areas. Every house we looked at had designated storage areas. In the LDS homes, the organization was impressive. Some had laminated lists with quantities and dates. I had never seen anything like it.

The food storage intrigued me, initially. Then I began to feel uncomfortable. I can't articulate why because I have nothing against stockpiling. My dad (not LDS) was a stickler for general readiness—he always had a solid plan and a safe "out." Organization and preparedness are in my blood. Maybe the Mormon version of food storage seemed extreme, or maybe I didn't like pondering any apocalyptic catastrophe, let alone what the Second Coming of Christ might look like. (People jumped on the food-and-water storage bandwagon during the Y2K scare, but efforts were willy-nilly, not so methodical.)

As we continued to walk through houses, I chose to look at the under-porch storage as the perfect wine cellar and looked past, what at the time, seemed to be zealot-like preparedness. It took me a couple of years before I realized that we couldn't live in a better place in the event of a natural, national, or biblical emergency. Our neighbors would no doubt feed us, and we in turn would be happy to take the edge off if they chose to partake of our wine.

Diversity Concerns

The more meticulously organized storage areas I saw, the more concerned I became about how and where we would find non-LDS neighbors and friends. I asked people—the Realtors, the loan officer, builders, sub-contractors, Target employees—something I never had before…"Are you LDS?"

Since our arrival in Utah, we had been asked several times if we were LDS or "members." I wasn't offended, but the question surprised me. In a day and age when asking someone's religion is generally considered inappropriate and should be irrelevant, I wasn't sure how to answer. I felt like there might be a right or wrong reply depending on who was asking. I wanted to say, "I am if you are," or "I'm not if you're not." I was convinced the social norm in the area deemed the question okay and relevant. And frankly, I wanted to know also.

I continued to ask people, when appropriate (which was probably never), if they were LDS. And guess what? The majority of people were, or they had been raised LDS and were taking a sabbatical (more on that later). On our weeklong house-hunting trip, I didn't meet many people, but I don't recall meeting one nonmember.

The Bottom Line

The fact that Salt Lake County is more religiously diverse than Utah County is common knowledge in the state. We were aware of the general Mormon migratory patterns, but we were not aware of the literal Point-Of-The-Mountain-Boundary and what it signified. Loosey-goosey Mormons (politically blue) on one side, by-the book Mormons (politically red) on the other.

Generally Speaking...

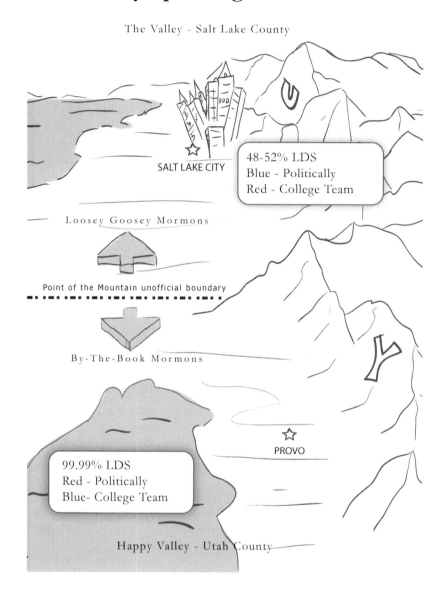

The Valley - Salt Lake County

SALT LAKE CITY

48-52% LDS
Blue - Politically
Red - College Team

Loosey Goosey Mormons

Point of the Mountain unofficial boundary

By-The-Book Mormons

PROVO

99.99% LDS
Red - Politically
Blue- College Team

Happy Valley - Utah County

We began our home search in Salt Lake County knowing it is considered more diverse, but we didn't find a place that excited us. We broadened our search to Utah County. Because Chris' job was in Provo, we chose to look at homes in a small town his co-workers recommended. They said the community was beautiful, clean, located equidistant from Salt Lake City and Provo, and because we love biking, running and hiking, we should check it out.

The town was beautiful! We found a great spec home and the school district seemed solid. Realtors avoid questions about religious demographics, and I didn't want to offend anyone, but I was concerned that our family might be the only nonmembers in the area. My attempts to uncover percentages of the member/nonmember population—were we looking at 80/20, 70/30, 60/40?—were handled with kid gloves. I expected to find more members of the Church than nonmembers but I wanted a SWAG at some numbers.

"So, just out of curiosity, are there many people around here who aren't Mormon?" I finally asked.

The Realtors, both the seller's and ours, looked at each other and took turns speaking.

"This is a lovely community!" "The arts are so valued." "You won't believe the elementary school concerts." "The high school productions are practically professional." "This is a special place." "There's no other place like it." "Oprah Winfrey is building a house here."

Because of the diplomatic answers to my question, we believed that although heavily LDS, this community was one of the more diverse in Utah County. We had found a liberal arts-loving, broad-minded, unique pocket of life. Even Oprah, apparently, recognized the specialness of our little Utah County town.

> NOTE: Mayberry, where we live, is not religiously diverse. Unless you consider diversity to include the fact that within the 99.99% LDS population here, there are a few families with only three children (by choice), there are two single mothers in the area, and I've occasionally seen people in church clothes at Costco on Sundays. Chris and I certainly wouldn't have avoided buying a house in our neighborhood had we known, but I would have let go of my plan to find enough friends to start a monthly wine-tasting club. (Something I'd enjoyed in a prior neighborhood.)

Regardless, we found a lovely home in a stunningly beautiful setting. We were aware of the "predominant faith," but were excited about the diversely blended culture described to us: the culture that focused on the arts, the love of outdoor activities, and the appreciation of nature. Our personal values and parenting style are "old fashioned." My prior experience with LDS friends in other states—friends who came from large, loving Osmond-like families with polite, well-behaved children who did their homework, and who enjoyed lots of laughter, success, and all-around good looks—led me to believe the community we found would be the perfect place for our family. A quasi-urban-granola couple, with strong family values and an appreciation for purposeful and vigilant parenting should fit in well, even if only 40, 30 or worst-case 20 percent of the population were nonmembers.

The neighborhood was new and slowly filling in. More transient families, like us, would be arriving and I would surely make new friends: both LDS gals and the wine- and coffee-drinking gals, too.

We purchased the house, and the boys and I returned to Colorado for a month to prepare for the move. I showed friends and family photos of our nearly finished home and the gorgeous surrounding mountains. I couldn't wait to join Chris and begin our lives in Utah.

So, the short answer to the question "How did you end up *here?*"—a community well known for the 99.99% LDS demographic?

We didn't know it was *that* Mormon. It was an accident.

History & Honeymoon

Phoenix, Arizona, 1979:

"I heard Mrs. Maxwell talking with her friend while I was babysitting. They kept calling people Brother-this and Sister-that," I told my mother. I was 14 years old.

"The Maxwells are Mormon and Mormons refer to each other as 'Brother' and 'Sister'," my mom explained.

"Why?"

"Well, they believe they're all brothers and sisters in their church." She didn't sound too sure.

"That's weird."

My mother, a bleeding heart liberal, said, "Christina. We don't say 'weird.' That's derogatory. We say 'different'."

"Kind of like the little hats the Jewish men wear?"

"Yes. Like that."

○●○

My Mormon Foundation

I was raised in a social melting pot. Religion didn't play a role in any of my friendships. There were Catholic, Jewish, Mormon, agnostic and atheist kids, all forming relationships based on common interests. Segregation occurred only on Sundays.

The Mormon kids I knew in the 70s and 80s throughout my middle and high school years were typically the "good" kids. I remember a couple of opposing teenage LDS boys but their indiscretions paled in comparison to the real bad boys. I recall one shotgun wedding, but happiness prevailed and the children were beautiful, naturally.

As an adult prior to moving to Utah, I had an occasional LDS coworker or neighbor; Chris had an LDS boss. Mormonism has never been an issue for Chris or me. Again, both of us have lived and worked in religiously diverse settings.

The knowledge that more Mormons than non-Mormons populated Utah didn't overly concern us. We assumed we'd coexist harmoniously. Unfortunately, we hadn't banked on the fact that we'd be the only family coexisting in our neighborhood as nonmembers. The reality? Knowing Mormons as friends and colleagues in other states was not an accurate litmus test for our readiness to move to Utah County.

The Honeymoon

Culture shock is expected when a person moves to another country, acclimates to a second language, or is not part of a dominant race. The symptoms were subtle, but I experienced classic culture shock.

I didn't recognize the encounter as a foreshadow at the time, but within a few weeks of settling into our home, an amiable neighbor couple stopped by to introduce themselves, welcome us to the community and bring a Christmas gift. (The first of many. We were indoctrinated into the phenomenon that is "Neighbor Gifts" during "The Season" in Utah.) They wished us a Merry Christmas and added, "We hope you like the *culture* here."

My parents were visiting from Arizona for the holidays, and my dad specifically noted the comment. "What did they mean by that?" he asked. I told him I wasn't sure, and then we all became distracted by the stream of neighbor gifts that followed for days leading up to Christmas. Incredible.

The Honeymoon Phase of culture shock is just like it sounds. Everything is wonderful! I loved everyone and everyone loved me. I'm a stay-at-home mom; so were most of the women I met. I like to cook, quilt and exercise. Score again. I even found a woman who hated scrapbooking, just like me. Neighbors were happy, friendly, and ever so helpful. *Good people.* And many had lived in other states so they went out of their way to acknowledge they were "new" to the area, too.

I enjoyed learning things about the Church. My LDS lingo was rapidly expanding. Every time someone used a word I wasn't familiar with, I simply asked and without exception the person gladly explained. I learned about Church callings, Primary, Young Women's, meetinghouse, the priesthood, visiting teachers, companions, general conference, fast

Sunday, Family Home Evening and Relief Society. Learning about the culture in my new neighborhood was novel, for the most part.

I read the *Book of Mormon* shortly before moving to Utah and although I did not convert, I found myself wanting to pretend I was a member. Kind of like it's fun to adopt a Southern accent in Texas, use the hang loose sign ad nauseam in Hawaii or order Mexican food with broken English. The reality is I was born and raised in the Midwest. No real southern accent, not a beach-y Hawaiian girl, no el-speak-o el-Spanish-o, and not a Mormon. But I enjoyed faking it in the Utah County McDonald's Playland, visiting with the other mothers (all much younger than me) while our kids played on the filthy equipment.

I never lied about not being a member; I just chose not to correct someone when they made the assumption that I was. How did I know I was perceived to be LDS? People used The Lingo with me. For example, while watching our children run around a fast-food play area, a woman I'd never met, but became intimate friends with for 47 minutes because that's what lonely stay-at-home mothers do, would casually mention her desire to be released from a calling. I sympathetically shook my head and acknowledged how difficult it is to balance the needs of our homes with our good intentions to serve. (I taught Sunday School at our church—briefly, because it almost killed me—so I was sincere.)

Occasionally a sub-contractor finishing up work in our house or on our yard called me Sister Ross. I liked it. I felt like I was in the club, in the know, one of the cool kids.

"How are you today, Sister Ross?" the clean-cut, young landscape worker asked me with a smile.

"Great!" I happily answered, still in disbelief that a place like Mayberry existed.

Then almost overnight, the honeymoon was over. We all hate when that happens, but it's a part of life. About six months after we'd moved into our home, the luster that surrounded all things Mormon, homemade and wholesome began to fade.

My focus shifted to our Realtors as an epiphany hit me. They had duped us.

Irritation & Paranoia

The Super Shuttle pulled away. My mother had arrived. "It's beautiful here," she said, "but it feels… funny."

I nodded.

"The driver asked me where I was from and what brought me to Utah. I told him I was here to help you with the kids. He said he lived in Provo and he asked me," her expression shifted, "Are you a member?'"

"Hm. Usually they just say, 'Are you LDS?'"

"It took me a minute to realize what he meant. He was from England and he moved here so he could be closer to BYU. He said he was a recent convert."

"Was he old?" I asked.

"He was probably in his 50s."

"I've heard the middle-aged adult converts can be the kookiest. Did he try to convert you?"

"I don't think so, but he seemed surprised that I wasn't Mormon, and even more surprised that you and Chris weren't Mormon. He was intense."

"I told you we live in one of the most Mormon areas of Utah. When I tell people here where we live, they say, 'Oh, that's Happy Valley.'" I continued, "You'll feel plenty of vibes here. Wait till we go to the grocery store. It's totally Mormony."

"Why?"

"Hardly any impulse buys near the check-out and they're usually LDS baptism cards and family job charts. Magazines are covered with a black plastic shield if the woman isn't wearing a 'Little House on the Prairie' dress. And you'll overhear people talk about mission letters, church callings and the bishop. It feels like a different world."

"I bet the bakery's good..."

I nodded.

○●○

The "Crisis Phase" or the "Negotiation Phase" in culture shock follows the high of living somewhere new. The gist is that a person feels frustrated and irritated by the new culture simply because it's different. On the surface, life in our new community appeared similar to life in other American towns. But the subtle, and not so subtle, differences were beginning to bother me.

It also became clear that diversity of any kind was a myth, and religious diversity was a joke.

Our neighborhood continued to slowly fill in with new families. I was surprised that a handful of people had been neighbors prior in nearby towns. I felt like Gladys Kravitz as I looked out our windows, sizing up the new folks unloading boxes from trucks, or walking by on the sidewalk. It became a game searching for one family like us: new, from out-of-state, and not Mormon.

A few times I thought, "This might be the one; they're from Minnesota; he went to graduate school in Boston; they have only three kids." My hopes were always shattered. *D'oh! They met at BYU. Damn.* It never failed.

I became acutely aware of how Mormon the community was. At the local grocery store my ears only heard The Lingo, my eyes only saw *LDS Living* and the black, plastic rectangle that protected our eyes from the scantily clad women on the cover of *Cosmopolitan*. (I actually think that's a great idea. Kids are eroticized too early in my opinion, but I had never seen fashion magazines obscured in markets in any other places.)

At the same grocery store, I shamelessly stared at strangers' arms and thighs looking for evidence of garments. If only I could find one woman with a real panty line problem. Occasionally I spotted someone wearing a sleeveless shirt, or the true mark of a nonmember, a cross. Unfortunately after closer inspection, the stranger in the cereal aisle whom I'd targeted to be my new nonmember friend appeared… rough around the edges. Where were the "normal" people who weren't LDS?

We decided to send our kids to a private school in Salt Lake County located 25 miles from our home. We were sold on the school's liberal arts curriculum and felt the diversity our sons would likely experience was worth the financial and logistical sacrifice.

While making the thirty-minute drive home from school, it became my routine to count steeples once I turned off the freeway onto the long road that took us deeper into Utah County. My eyes scanned left and right; my lips moved like "Rain Man's" as I counted; the kids asked me if I was talking to myself again; and I became annoyed as the number increased. When I spotted a new church being built, it made me angry. How many more churches do these people need? Do they all have seven children? They're multiplying like crazy. The steeples didn't affect me directly; they were a reminder of the reality that I was not a thread in the cultural fabric of my community.

> NOTE: Years later, to this day, when friends or family visit us from out of state, they almost always comment on the number of steeples they see as we drive from the freeway toward our house. I don't even notice anymore.

I was beginning to feel oppressed. And paranoid.

Just Because You're Paranoid…

I was periodically invited to Relief Society activities. Once I understood what Relief Society meant—a sorority for nice, married, sober girls—I asked an LDS friend who lived outside of "our ward" boundaries if my attendance would send the wrong message. I was hungry for friendship but not interested in conversion. My friend told me if I ultimately was not interested in converting that the invitations would likely cease. "Relief Society activities are for LDS women and I'm afraid if you don't join the Church, they'll probably stop including you."

She wasn't trying to convert me; I believe she was trying to answer my question honestly. Her answer discouraged me from attending Relief Society activities for the first few years, even though other women told me I was welcome regardless.

During the height of my paranoia, I was suspicious that any attempts to befriend me were rooted in church obligations and not genuine friendship. One day a neighbor knocked on my door to invite me to a Relief Society function (again). This was a gal I thought I had things in common with outside of our faiths. I said, "If you're inviting me because you think I'll enjoy myself or you believe we have things in common as women, neighbors, wives, mothers and hopefully friends, then I'm open. If I'm just a missionary opportunity, my feelings are hurt."

I wanted to socialize with other women, but I wasn't convinced that Relief Society invitations were offered with no strings attached. My new "friends" would surely liquor me up on lemonade, sugary baked goods, white rolls and real butter. "Forget the crafts, brainwash Chris! Roll out the pool! Dunk her!"

My neighbor didn't know what to say after my spiel. I'm sure I hurt her feelings—not my intention—but I was confused. Every social gathering was driven by ward boundaries. This was new to me. I began to believe that the only way to be accepted and interact with other women was to become a Mormon. (So I did. And we all lived happily ever after. The end… Kidding.)

Because of my personal revelation—the way to fit in and find friendship was conversion—I further tormented myself by wearing an uncomfortable Mormon-filter. Perhaps if I projected an I'm-LDS-Like vibe, women would cut me some slack. Even though my basic personality and mothering style was old-fashioned, and Chris and I went to bed earlier and were quieter than many of our neighbors, I felt compelled to portray a Sandra Dee meets Martha Stewart meets Earth Muffin image. Not completely disingenuous, because a part of me likes the idea, but a stretch for any person.

I was annoyed by the Mormon-ness of everyone, yet I desired to be liked. I worried the neighbors wouldn't let their kids come over to play if we had a coffee maker on the counter, beer in the refrigerator, or visible contraband of any kind.

When the doorbell rang in the evening and I had a glass of wine poured, internal sirens blared in my head. I was like a running back, shoving my kids out of the way so I could hide the glass in a cabinet, grab a piece of gum and fluff my hair before answering the door. Trying to hide anything is exhausting. I felt tired, frustrated and lonely. I wanted to "get it off me"—the feeling that I was in a place that I didn't belong and that I couldn't be me. The reality? Not one person shamed me for being me. These were my own self-imposed thoughts and restrictions.

Church Par-tay

It was odd to me that almost all social events were church-driven, not neighborhood- or relationship-driven. As ward boundaries changed, so did relationships. It felt like an "It's not you, it's me," break-up. Women who befriended me initially, drifted away when the boundary changed. My paranoia was further fueled.

As much as I sometimes resented invitations to church activities, there were times within the first few years of our landing in Mayberry, I believed we were conspicuously excluded from events. I now know that it was an innocent oversight, an LDS specific event not appropriate for a nonmember, or it was a deliberate decision not to make us feel like the Church was smothering or trying to convert us. My husband had an experience with a man in our neighborhood who candidly said, "My wife and I struggle with when and how often to invite you guys to stuff. We don't want you to feel like we're going to sneak up behind you with a bucket of water and baptize you."

I felt slighted. I cried to my husband, "They don't want us living here. They may not be throwing rocks at our house, but we're not welcome." Mormons were damned if they did, *You don't reeeally want to be my friend; I'm just a missionary opportunity.* And damned if they didn't, *We're excluded again; it's like The Amityville Horror. They're hissing, "Get. Out."*

Everyone pretended like it didn't matter if the answer was "yes" or "no" to the question, "Are you LDS?" But the relevance was palpable, even if it was only a figment of my imagination.

I complained to my mother one day on the phone.

"I'm so lonely, Mom. I don't know how much longer I can live here. I think I'm depressed."

"Remember when your father and I lived in Venezuela? All I wanted was mustard on my sandwich. I couldn't figure out how to say 'mustard' in Spanish. Even though I was in a beautiful place with interesting people, I was tired, lonely and depressed. Know why? Culture shock, honey. You're experiencing culture shock. I expected it in another country. You just didn't see it coming."

Mom was right. I underestimated what at first seemed like interesting and understated differences within Mormon culture, were just that. Differences.

Moves are difficult. I've lived in six states; I'm familiar with move stress. Culture shock was new.

The Become-A-Jack-Mormon Plan

"You need to become a Jack Mormon," said Dad.

My parents were visiting from Arizona after I'd given birth to our third son in the fall of 2005. Dad arrived a few days after Mom and he was blown away when he learned about the nightly meals that Relief Society delivered to our home.

"A neighbor has brought you a meal every night for two weeks?" he asked in disbelief.

"Kaye?" he yelled to my mother who was in the other room holding the baby. "Have you ever heard of such a thing? Two weeks. They've had a hot meal delivered to the house every night for two weeks."

"I know," Mom replied. "They've been delicious."

"Chrisy said they even get dessert." Dad was amazed.

He looked at me, "What you need to do is join the Church. Say what you need to say, do all the ceremonial stuff, and then become a Jack Mormon. Once you're in, you can get all the perks. Then go back to drinking your wine and coffee. Just get it over with, and they won't try to convert you all the time. I'll ask my Mormon friend at the golf course about it."

○●○

There were times Dad's strategy appealed to me. The structure, organization and built-in support system within the ward were appealing. Neighborhoods I'd lived in prior, people helped one another, but this was an army of consistent and meaningful help. I'm an above average actress, but I knew I'd crack under the scrutiny of my excited LDS friends if I tried to pull off the Become-A-Jack-Mormon Plan.

Spastic Paranoia Before The Calm

During our second and third years living in Mayberry, my paranoia lurched and receded weekly. There had to be proof that some person or document was instructing people to insidiously make me feel lonely and universally pissed off at everything. I researched Church teachings, watched KBYU, and listened to or read general conference talks. A smoking gun did not exist. I realized my issues were cultural and personal, not doctrinal.

I toggled between believing that I was slowly making progress with new friendships, and disappointment when those friendships seemed to go dormant for long stretches. Most people parented a handful or two handfuls of children, had extended family living in the area, had well-established bonds, and all of those church responsibilities. Many women didn't have the time to squeeze in a new relationship. I followed the logic, but lonely feelings remained the result. Their dance cards were full. And I wanted to dance.

The Lingo that I proudly flaunted when I tried to fake Mormon began to irritate me. Mormonese appeared in all conversations. Instead of, "My husband's taking some boys on a bike ride," the language was, "My husband's riding bikes with the deacons." Another opportunity for me to learn more about the Priesthood as I raced home and googled like crazy.

Validation From The Salt Lake County Mormons

I became more comfortable talking about my feelings with friends I met at our sons' school; the private school they attended on the loosey-goosey Mormon side of Point of the Mountain (the dividing line between Salt Lake and Utah counties).

It was refreshing to see cars in the school parking lot with "CTR" bumper stickers parked next to cars with "Darwin Loves You" and "Coexist" stickers. Even though there was more religious diversity in Salt Lake County, I remained interested in who was and who wasn't LDS.

The first few times I saw an LDS mother in teeny, tiny workout clothes retrieving her children from school, I was stunned. *Is that against the rules? She's practically naked! And what a body! This scene would never play out at the public school near our home in Utah County. There must be different Mormon police in Salt Lake County, because these women would be so busted in my neck of the woods.*

One LDS friend said, "I don't know how you do it. I love the Church, but I can't stand the Mormon culture. Especially in Utah County. I like having different people in my neighborhood."

I was interested and surprised. "Really?"

"Sure. We have a neighborhood book club and it's a wide mix of people. I need variety. You should look for a house in our neighborhood. You'd fit in great."

I thought about what she said and remembered that she and her husband were getting ready to travel to Europe. "Keep me posted on houses in your neighborhood. And can you bring me some wine back from your trip?"

"Uh, no."

Mormons.

○●○

A few other LDS friends in Salt Lake County shared their thoughts. Utah County, although beautiful, was not their preferred vibe and they weren't even Democrats.

The validation of my feelings and experiences, the passing of time, and a few emerging friendships helped the funky-colored sky in my world begin to return to its trusty blue. I began to appreciate and value the predictable nature of our community. I enjoyed heading north to play with the loosey-goosey Mormons, mingle among some of my people at Starbucks, and have the option to buy a beer at a pizza parlor. But I felt a palpable "ahhh" when I returned home. It turns out that I liked feeling insulated.

Deacons, Young Men, Young Women—they were all just the neighbor kids. They were my babysitters, odd-job tacklers and my young friends. Ward boundaries changed—again—a Bishop was released, a new one was called, and my world wasn't knocked off its axis. Culture shock had run its course, I was comfortable in my own skin again, and I felt a sense of vindication when Salt Lake County Mormons raised their eyebrows upon learning where I lived. I wasn't crazy—I had acclimated to a sub-culture within a sub-culture within a culture (Utah County Mormons, as a subset of Utah Mormons, as a subset of Mormons), that even some of the LDS set found challenging.

Just How Mormon Is Our Community?

We're mistaken for an LDS family everywhere we go because of where we live. On the Jungle Cruise at Disneyland a few years ago, the tour guide asked where everyone was visiting from. When we told him Mayberry, Utah, he said, "I have relatives *there*." Then his eyes moved from my husband's to mine as he took conspicuous note of our three young boys sitting on the bench between us.

We passed the obvious and easy tests. More than two children and we were a young enough looking couple to produce more, my husband and I both wore short sleeve shirts—no tanks or camis—and knee-length shorts, we weren't carrying a to-go cup of coffee, and our family isn't particularly ugly. And so it was that the You're-Mormon-And-So-Am-I glance was exchanged between the Jungle Cruise guide and us. (Even though we're not LDS, it's easier to fake it in some situations.)

As the tour guide continued to entertain the boarding passengers, he joked how we likely had a trampoline in our backyard (we don't). I smiled and nodded vigorously when he asked about my ability to make funeral potatoes and Jell-O salads (I can't).

It doesn't matter where we are—Utah, or any other state or country—if we cross paths with a person who knows the town where we live, the assumption is that all parties involved are members. When we meet people in our own town for the first time, outside of our ward boundaries, they also assume we're Brother and Sister Ross. We understand. And it doesn't bother us…anymore.

When the time feels right, my husband or I reveal that we don't happen to be members of the Church, followed by an enthusiastic and honest, "…although we love living in our community!" People are typically gracious, but are also sincerely curious about our experience.

Occasionally, our presence has caught someone off guard and made them uncomfortable. One day, my husband was in the front yard on a sunny Saturday afternoon, fiddling with landscape lights, digging in the dirt, and keeping an eye on our five-year-old son. Our two older boys were running around the yard enjoying the pleasant weather. A car pulled into our driveway and a woman jumped out of the passenger side, approached Chris with a broad smile and asked, "What's the ward like here?"

My husband returned the smile and replied, "It's great! We don't happen to be LDS, but the neighborhood's super nice."

The woman said, "Oh," turned around, got back into the car, had a brief exchange with the man behind the wheel and they pulled out of the driveway, avoiding eye contact.

Chris said, "I think I spooked her."

People are almost always surprised to learn we're not members, but they're rarely spooked. I only share these examples to emphasize the Mormon-ness of our Mormon community.

One more case in point and then I'll shush.

A few years ago, I pulled my left quad leaping over our youngest son while I was hurrying down the stairs. I almost passed out from the pain. My three boys stared at me as I lay there making guttural noises, beads of sweat on my forehead. The small child I leaped over said, "You hurt you-self, Mom?"

There's a sports medicine guy in our town that everyone goes to. He's like the great and powerful Oz. You either see him, or amputate. I got in to see "the guy" immediately.

Apparently, a torn muscle, when treated ASAP after the injury, can heal miraculously fast.

After assessing my predicament The Guy made polite small talk. "So, you're a Ross." (*brow furrowed, thinking, thinking, thinking…*)

"Yes. I'm friends with Mary Ann and Ginger. They both recommended you."

He knew whom I was referring to. "Oh, you have the boy who's a senior." (*thinking, thinking, thinking…*)

"No. I have three boys—10, 8, and 2 1/2. I'm old enough to have a senior though." I laughed uncomfortably, knowing he was trying to place me within the Church context.

"What's your husband do?" (*thinking, thinking, thinking…*)

"He's a marketing guy. I don't really know what he does."

I wanted to put The Guy out of his misery and say: You don't know us because we're not in your ward. We're not in any ward. My boys aren't deacons. My husband's not on the bishopric and my calling is nada. We're **the** family, living on **that** corner, who are **not** members. Then The Guy could say, "OH. Those Rosses."

My therapy session was finished and a female intern was summoned to wrap my leg. The Guy explained that if I needed to go home to get underclothes they could wrap tightly over…anything. I said thank you, he left the room and the young woman entered to wrap my leg.

"Do you want me to just lift up my shorts?" I asked.

"No. You're going to have to remove them; I need to wrap this around your hips, too. If you need to put something else on before I wrap, I can wait."

"Just so you know, I'm not LDS. Before I pull my shorts down, I should also tell you I'm wearing green underwear with white polka dots. Sorry." I was mortified that my underwear would reveal my nonmember status. At least they were bottom-covering cotton and not the skimpy racy variety.

Smiling, the woman said, "You mean there are two of us in this town?"

I was surprised to learn that she wasn't LDS. She actually lived in a nearby town, but the religious demographics are the same in most Utah County towns. Coincidentally, I ran into her several months later, of all places, at the liquor store. Proof that some stereotypes exist for a reason.

The following day I returned to see the wonderful sports medicine guy. I was treated, and again it was time for my wrap. He was still struggling to place my husband, our family and me. "Okay, time to get wrapped. I know you live close so if you want to run home and get anything you need to wear for the day, we can wrap over that." (*thinking, thinking, thinking*...she seems nice enough to be Mormon???)

"Thanks. I'm good," I replied.

My leg was wrapped, I was given final instructions, and off I went.

As The Saying Goes

We often hear about difficult things, "There's no way around it, you have to go through it." Somewhere between three and four years after our arrival to Mayberry, it ceased to be the Mormon community where I lived, and it became, simply, my home. That's not to say that I didn't continue to experience reminders of the fact that we live in a well-defined culture that we're not intimately a part of. But, I no longer bristled, became offended, nor felt the need to defend where our family lived. Loud and proud, I say, "We live in Mayberry!" And sadly for my dad, we're still not Jack Mormons.

PART II

Observations

The Kids

"Johnny said we're not real Christians if we're not Mormon," my then second-grader reported one day after school.

"Well, Johnny's confused. I'm sure he doesn't know what he's saying. What did you say?"

"Nothing."

"That's probably best. And just so you know, there are several varieties of Christians."

"Johnny also said that Catholics don't pay their taxes."

"Oh. That happens to be true."

(I didn't really say that.)

○●○

An interesting fact occurred to me after a few years of living in Mayberry, Utah County, Utah. Although many local adults had lived in other states and attended graduate school at institutions other than BYU, the children of these adults had been born and raised (so far) in our insulated community. Broad minded LDS parents who desired to raise their children in a Mormon community—understandably—were raising kids who, to date, had limited exposure to life outside of Happy Valley. Their world was 99% Mormon, probably by design, but I hadn't thought about the ramifications of that fact for our kids.

Neighborhood kids entered our home, no doubt coached by their parents to behave well, use their manners and be tolerant of nonmember ways. Their little eyes widened when they saw a decorative cross hanging on the wall in our home, or the coffee maker in the kitchen. It was interesting to observe.

Many of these children have traveled more than my husband and I have combined, but their day-to-day lives, their world, was Mormon. All of it.

One Sunday our sons were playing outside and asked a few neighbor kids to join. "We can't. It's the Sabbath," they said in a scolding tone.

Our sons were confused. Our family had been to church, it was a pretty day, and so they didn't understand why they couldn't play with their friends. Chris and I were given the opportunity for teachable moment number 5,000 out of infinity. We've since learned, as have our sons, that Mormon families differ in what they deem appropriate Sabbath activity.

We tried to educate our kids on Mormonism, basic principles, traditions, and the surface differences. They seemed to follow what we said, but ultimately were most impressed with the golden Angel Moroni on top of the temple. It fascinated them and still does.

Scouts

Our sons had difficulty finding time to bond with neighbor kids. We all know friendships can't be forced. Sometimes they happen and sometimes they don't. Add the extra hurdles of attending different schools and not crossing paths at Church functions, and chances to create a "shared experience history" and connect with others is even more of a struggle. Navigating the new cultural waters in Utah County and finding time to cultivate friendships was complex for me as an adult. I didn't think about my kids sailing the same choppy waters. The situation was unique.

A friend suggested our sons join Cub Scouts locally. We were sold on the wholesome activities and goals. I was concerned about my sons being the only nonmembers and asked the Scout leader to help minimize any exclusionary feelings. The curiosity from other children about our family not being Mormon was already palpable. It was important to us that our sons not feel uncomfortable about the way they prayed if called on to perform the opening prayer before a meeting. Our family had observed our LDS friends pray. We saw people cross their arms and heard the words "Heavenly Father", "thee", "thy", and "thou." Our kids clasped their hands or held hands with the person standing next to them and toggled between, "Father", "Lord", and "God", but usually they just talked to "God." Their language was reverent but conversational.

The Scout leader said she called the other parents to give them a heads up about the situation. As parents, we all supported one another and our kids. I feel everyone did their best to educate the boys on religious differences. My sons declined the offer to say the opening prayer every time it was extended to them. They said they never felt comfortable and were nervous because they didn't pray like "everyone else." My concern had been realized despite our best efforts to minimize the slight disparity. Kids have keen senses.

I didn't recognize that my sons were joining LDS Scouts. It gets a little tricky, but there's Boy Scouts of America, and then there's LDS Boy Scouts of America. My sons joined LDS Scouts. The differences were subtle enough while they were young so the experience was worthwhile, but eventually The Lingo and Church goals (an LDS Mission for example) dominated Scout events and gatherings. When our boys expressed their desire to quit after a couple of years, we gently pushed for their reasons. They expressed the usual, *we're bored, we're tired, the boys are rowdy*, and *we're not doing anything fun*. But we believe it boiled down to the fact that the experience simply became too "different." They weren't deacons.

> NOTE TO NONMEMBERS: LDS Scouts is basically the same as Boy Scouts of America, but suffice to say LDS boys share a common goal— mission papers. If a wayward LDS boy chooses not to pursue his Eagle Scout Award, LDS parents

begin to worry that he might be off mission-papers trajectory. LDS Scouts has a decidedly Mormon bent, hence the name.

There are discussions in some wards about whether it's appropriate or worthwhile to invite nonmember boys into the LDS Scout program. This offended me at first, but I understand the importance of the goals and expectations for the LDS Scouting program and why the program is chartered under the Boy Scouts of America specific to Church needs. There's also the issue of tithing. The people in our ward (see how comfortable I am referring to "our ward") have always been gracious and generous. Every time we tried to pay for anything Scout related, we were told the expense was already covered. I imagine in communities where there are more nonmember boys, the ward would have to address the financial issues that go along with inviting others to participate.

○●○

The Cub Scouts were making homemade drums. I sent my son to his meeting with an empty coffee can.

"Why do you have a coffee can?" one boy asked my son.

"My parents drink coffee."

"Mormons don't drink coffee," said the boy.

"We're not Mormon," my son replied.

And that was that—for my son. Although, later that day, my son came home and asked me *why* Mormons don't drink coffee. He also expressed concern about his father's and my daily coffee consumption. Thanks, Mormon boy. As a family, we experienced teachable moment number 5,001 out of infinity. We addressed the whole alcohol thing while we were on the topic of beverages. It had never occurred to me to talk with my six- and eight-year-old sons about coffee, tea and wine.

Somehow we found the words to explain the beliefs and choices on each side of the coin, without casting judgment. It's not wrong or bad for people to choose not to put certain things in their bodies. And it's not wrong or bad for your parents to put those very things (that in excess might be bad) in our bodies. We're free to hit ourselves in the head with a hammer! All of us!

In an effort to not make the rule sound extreme, I made my husband and myself look like reckless idiots. Then I had a glass of wine. And I told my sons that Diet Coke is poison.

When Scouts ended, I can't say that I shed a tear.

The Naughty Ones

I almost giggle. Overall the kids in our area are Eddie Haskell polite. If they're ornery, they hide their behavior from the eyes and ears of adults. Something I'm completely in favor of. I rarely see graffiti. And the graffiti that I have seen, however rare, is almost shockingly wholesome. In fact, the foulest word I've seen has five letters, is mildly vulgar and begins with "d". (If the kid who wrote it is like me, neither one of us is entirely sure of its meaning or usage.)

○●○

Our house was toilet-papered one night a few years ago. I'm certain it was random. We're a corner house—adjacent to a park—so it was an easy attack and escape. My parents, who were visiting at the time from Arizona (again), witnessed the infraction.

Dad was on it. He was up a few hours before the rest of us. "Your house was TP'd last night," Dad informed me. "I almost tripped on my way out to get the paper. They wrapped plastic wrap around your timbers."

I walked to the front windows to see what Dad was talking about. And what did I see? A dozen or more teenagers cleaning the mess in our yard. I recognized one of the girls and called her mother.

"Katie saw your yard and was afraid you and your family would feel targeted. The Young Women and Young Men were getting together this morning for a Mutual activity so it was convenient for them to work on the mess," said my friend.

I was moved by Katie's desire to protect and help us. I appreciated all of those kids cleaning our yard, especially when my oldest child was eight, and my kids would be of little or no help. I showed Dad.

"I bet you a few of those kids who are cleaning are the ones who TP'd," said Dad. "Now the kids are after you. You better just convert." He was still campaigning for the Become-A-Jack-Mormon Plan.

Who knows, but I doubted it.

The Park

As I mentioned earlier, we live adjacent to a park. In some towns, living across the street from a park is a detriment. Not here.

During baseball season we hear the crack of the bat on a sunny afternoon. Families take evening walks or bike rides along the park paths, pausing a moment to allow a young child to throw rocks in the creek. Older couples walk hand in hand daily, sometimes dragging a little dog and its tank of oxygen behind them. Evening gatherings end when it gets dark, and there is no loud music or lewd and drunken behavior. It's bizarrely idyllic. Except around graduation.

Every spring without fail, high school kids congregate at the park for a night or two of graduation celebrating. (Maybe I should enroll myself in the Witness Protection Program before I continue. I'm about to out myself as the killjoy who calls the police.) I try to be cool, thinking, "Aw. The Mormon kids are partying. How cute."

As a teenager I pledged to be a hip adult, promising to remember and understand teen angst and support a young person's journey, within reason. Turns out I'm a jerk.

○●○

"It's 10:30. I say we call the cops."

"My how you've changed since we first met and danced in a park late at night with friends," Chris replied.

"They've got to have alcohol over there. I see at least 50 cars and the music is shaking the house. Ridiculous. I'm calling."

Disappointed, my husband hands me the phone.

"Hi. Chris Ross again. The kids are back. I know they're just looking for a place to hang out, and I can't see any alcohol, but the noise is terrible. We have young children trying to sleep. I'm sorry."

"No problem, Mrs. Ross."

"Am I the only one who's called?"

"Yes. It's usually just you."

"Please don't share that with anyone."

The cops show up, the kids scramble for their cars, and they crank their music as they tear out of the park, wildly honking their horns. Bad Mormon kids.

This scene plays out every spring at least once and no more than three times. I should post a flyer at the local high schools, reminding students that they will not successfully gather at the park across the street from our house, because the only uncool parent in the neighborhood happens to also be the only nonmember. And that parent will call the cops. Go figure.

The Thing About Seminary

"Are you sure that's not on school property?" I asked a girlfriend as we jogged past a high school on our morning run. She assured me the LDS seminary building was on property owned by the Church.

What a coincidence that the Church owns property adjacent to almost all public junior high and high schools. The kids only have to walk 15 yards to attend seminary class, which coincidentally is available to them during the middle of the day. How convenient.

Forgive my sarcasm. It bothered me at first, but it doesn't anymore. My LDS friends have shared how difficult it was living in other states, getting kids to 6:30 a.m. (or earlier) seminary, sometimes located in a strip mall, and then delivering kids to school on time. If I were a Mormon person, I would desire an LDS seminary building a stone's throw away from my child's school. And I would desire that I not have to get up in the middle of the night to get my child to seminary class. The logic is easy to follow. One small space in a strip mall wouldn't be large enough for the number of kids in the Utah public school system that attend seminary. The majority of the people in my community see nothing unusual about a religious building sitting like a little red-bricked cherry on top of their child's middle or high school. I digress.

The word on the street among nonmembers was that the isolation felt during mid-day seminary periods was hard on nonmember students in middle and high school. I worried about how my children would feel when they had to deal with this unique dynamic, but it was all for naught. Because the school our sons attend is a private liberal arts school, all religious classes, clubs and meetings occur outside of normal school hours. The same as when my husband and I were in high school.

I haven't had to parent through the challenges of my nonmember child being only one of a handful of students not attending LDS seminary. Therefore, I can't say it's been an issue for our family. I don't have a problem with an LDS seminary building located adjacent to campus when the majority of the students are LDS. However it's difficult to reconcile the isolation the nonmember kids might feel during the middle of the school day if they choose not to partake of the seminary class. I recognize all students are more than welcome to attend. It's complicated.

The Dating Game

I asked my hair stylist at the time, a young newly married Mormon gal, about kids, seminary and dating prospects for our sons. She was as fascinated by our nonmember status in the community as I was about all things Mormon. The candid young woman told me most nonmembers that move to our community "hate Mormons" and smoke cigarettes on their front porch. She said, "It's like they hate us and hate living here. I don't know why they stay." I believed her.

"Will our boys be able to date girls from around here when they're teenagers?" I asked my hair stylist.

"Probably not. A lot of people only let their kids group date and if they do let their daughter go on a date-date… they'll want her to date a Mormon boy," she replied honestly.

Like the seminary situation, it stung a bit, but I understood. I recall hearing the parents of my Jewish and Catholic friends expressing the desire for their sons and daughters to marry a nice Jewish girl or boy. The same can be said for some (not all) agnostic, born-again Christian, Hindu, and even atheist parents. Again, the logic isn't complicated. I still winced at the thought of my sons feeling slighted and overlooked by their peers because they weren't Mormon. In the same breath, if dates were a means of shopping for spouses, I pass on behalf of my sons. I don't particularly want them dating until they graduate from college.

We're in the perfect place.

A Glimmer Of Hope For My Mormon Friends

The BYU and University of Utah rivalry is big. Parents begin preparing their children for the college of choice with the dedication and discipline of church lessons. Politics comes next. Our sons started bringing home Ute and BYU jokes in the second grade. They reported that the kids on the playground engaged in smacktalk and already knew which college they planned to attend.

First, my sons wanted to know what "college" was. We explained that college was *their* mission.

My eight-year-old son informed us, with his six-year-old brother planted firmly beside him and nodding in agreement, "Well, we're going to BYU. And we're never drinking alcohol."

No. We don't live in Utah.

As Bad As It Gets

And *that* is about as bad as the kids get here in Mayberry.

Mormons On Sabbatical

"Is she drinking a real martini? It's pink so it could be a virgin cocktail," I said to my nonmember friend at the Ladies Night Out dinner for mothers from our kids' school.

"It's real. She's drinking a cosmopolitan. And watch her. She'll drink five or six more and someone's going to have to drive her home," replied my friend.

"I can't watch. She was such a good Mormon."

I was physically uncomfortable watching a middle-aged woman, who up until recently had been an active member of the Church, get tanked. She was sitting far enough away from me that I could observe and not directly interact with her.

"She's swearing now! Does her husband know about this?" I asked.

"I think he's on his way to the dark side, too."

○●○

Not all Mormons on sabbatical depart in a string of midlife binge drinking parties. But I'm surprised at the number of inactive LDS people who party like fraternity boys. The sabbatical continuum ranges from those who dipped their big toe in the water *once* a long time ago, in and out and inners, quiet underwater types, to surface swimmers who splash and make noise so there's no doubt in anyone's mind that the person is taking a leave.

Touched It With My Big Toe…Once

I'm usually correct when I assume my LDS friends (especially the ones who live in my neighborhood—the Utah County Mormons) have never been intoxicated, smoked a cigarette or sipped a cup of coffee. Occasionally I felt it was my duty to explain a slice of life from the dark side. These conversations are painful to recall because number one; I didn't need to explain anything, and number two; I didn't need to speak slowly or loudly.

"I had a couple of glasses of wine with dinner last night. Feeling a little sluggish this morning," I inform my morning running partners. "Even had hot pipes in the middle of the night. You girls probably don't know what those are," I say patronizingly. "It's when you wake up in the middle of the night, dreaming you're swimming with your mouth open, because you're so thirsty. Then you get up and drink tons of water."

My friends politely courtesy laugh, and throw in a, "Hmmm." Nobody cares about hot pipes, and if they already knew about them, they certainly wouldn't divulge the fact on a *group* run.

However, on occasion someone does share that they too have experienced hot pipes, or tried a cigarette, or had a cup of coffee. Just once or twice when they were young, experimenting and confused, mumble, mumble. Sometimes the person alludes to their transgression, other times they provide dates, details and are comfortable purging the story once more.

I have no lifelong convictions rooted in religion, so I prefer not to compare and contrast my behaviors with those of my LDS friends. However, I relate the most to this personality type—the Big-Toe-Dipper—because I too broke a few rules when I was younger. It happens.

In-And-Out-And-Inners

Are we in or are we out folks? These people make me the most uncomfortable. Once I've learned someone has chosen to go inactive, I process the information and file it accordingly. Over the years I've encountered a few people who occasionally partake of obvious contraband, only to observe those same people rid themselves of tank tops and revert to virgin daiquiris. A few months later I see a little more skin and witness alcohol consumption, then a few months after that, cap-sleeves and cream soda.

This happens with people in other religions, but for some reason, it troubles me more to witness an LDS person struggle with commitment to their faith. My personal double standard might stem from the fact that the rules and expectations are clear for certain Mormon observable behaviors. We all struggle at times with doubt about many things, but there's not always an outward sign of the spin cycle that occurs in our heads.

I feel uncomfortable, and a little motion sick, watching the waffler. Which is ironic, because I'm notorious for seeing and empathizing with both sides of an issue.

Quiet Underwater Swimmers

"You guys live in Mayberry?" a new friend from my sons' school asked me. We were at a child's party.

"Yes."

"Are you LDS?" she asked.

"No."

"Wow. That's interesting. I was raised in Salt Lake City, and Mayberry's beautiful, but I think it would be difficult to live there."

I didn't know her very well, but wouldn't have placed her in the LDS camp. By this time, it was reasonable to assume when someone said they were raised in Utah, it was code for, "I'm LDS."

"It works for us," I said. "We ride bikes and run, and the neighborhood is great. Are you LDS?"

"I was raised LDS, but my husband isn't. He grew up in California." Her answer didn't exactly answer my question, so I was left wondering about her story.

Over the years I learned that she, like a few others I've met, slowly and quietly left the Church. There wasn't a public flameout, nor was there a loud mockery of the Church. These people might share their thoughts privately if asked. And they don't typically party like a fraternity boy. They can hold their liquor, and it doesn't have to be sugar sweet.

When Underwater Swimmers surface, they sidestroke. There's simply not much of a splash.

Splashers

We've all seen the Splashers. I've heard there's one in every family. Doesn't matter if the person is male, female, 18 or 48. The drinking of fruity alcohol-laden drinks in large quantities, carrying Starbucks cups as a constant reminder of who they no longer are and clothing that's not garment friendly are all dead giveaways.

"Time for a cup o' Joe!" a Splasher might deliberately announce. As someone who's always been a nonmember and enjoys coffee, we don't always announce our coffee consumption intentions, and "cup o' Joe" is a little dorky. We also don't binge drink every time we drink alcohol. Fraternity boys and alcoholics binge drink. There are people who consume adult beverages responsibly. I promise.

Female Splashers are fond of tank tops and camis. Spring, summer, winter, and fall are all appropriate skin-baring seasons for these gals. It's like they want to scream, "Look! I'm not wearing garments!"

We know. We see. You're also holding a giant Starbucks cup. You're not active, and I'm sure you'll remind everyone for the rest of your life. Splash all you want, fun folks. Just don't get me wet. Makes me arch my back.

Honorable Mention: Posers

It takes one to know one. As a person who has quasi-posed as a member of the LDS Church, I feel comfortable calling out a scene that my husband and I have both witnessed. Active members, who don't cross hard lines with their behavior, but seem to enjoy mingling among those who do.

Just like my pathetic attempt at faking Mormon, there are some people who fake non-Mormon. They enjoy attending parties dominated by nonmembers, laugh loudly at crass jokes, drop a few swear words, wear the latest fashions, hold a club soda with a lime wedge and avoid Mormonese. There's no question the Posers are dedicated to their faith, but there's also no doubt that they enjoy playing with an edgier set once in a while. I get it. I can go there. Because I have…and I do.

Two Disclosures

DISCLOSURE ONE: I'm jealous of Mormons on sabbatical. A person's prior active status, years of seminary, and completion of various rituals gives them a native-like position that I'll never have. An inactive person can party like a rock star on Friday night, then attend a family reunion in Idaho on Saturday, and feel comfortable in each social setting. I've watched active members grin with and dap (knocking fists together) their inactive family members and friends. It's like they're bilingual, and I'm not. They slip into and out of the fold easily.

DISCLOSURE TWO: I don't want to be complicit in someone's departure from the Church. The example at the beginning of this chapter made me very uncomfortable. It seemed like just the week prior, the woman who was drinking martinis had been a happy active Mormon gal and then overnight everything changed. Clearly deep and personal thoughts had been in her head for a while. Observing the transition stirred sadness in me, although I understand life transitions well. But I frankly don't want to buy someone a cup of coffee, offer them a glass of wine, or take them out shopping on Sunday, unless the person has been engaging in these behaviors for quite some time. (Rule-breaking is no stranger to me, so I feel like I'm talking out of both sides of my mouth.) Even though I'm not LDS, the thought of someone abandoning their long-standing beliefs and values takes me to a pensive place. I respect the path of personal growth we're all on, but don't ask me for an adult beverage if you've never had one. I can't handle the pressure.

Final Thoughts On the Sabbatical

I've had some fun at the expense of what is, I'm certain, a very personal and complicated experience for others. In all sincerity, I'm not judging the choices people make. I have a broad spectrum of friends who have gone through life changes and will continue to do so. And I would have *no* friends if they all judged me for the variety of life's outfits I've sported over the years. There are a few more hats I hope to wear. Nothing too crazy, but I would be heartbroken if relationships were lost over a silly hat.

Bonus Holiday, Neighbor Gifts & Power Parties

You Say Pioneers, I Say Pilgrims

"Why are those kids dressed like pilgrims?" I was on the phone with one of my neighbors as I watched a stream of kids in costumes walk by our house.

"They're getting home from their trek."

"Is this another Mormon thing?"

"Yes," she laughed. "The youth reenact the pioneer handcart trek." Then she explained the gist of the activity and answered my questions. The basics were covered.

I learned about the Ma's and the Pa's, the trials and the tragedies and the spiritual and personal growth the kids experience.

I became versed in the trek our first Utah summer. The endeavor sounded extreme, and like dry and cold storage, contributed a bit to my culture shock and gave me one more "freaky" thing to report to my parents when we talked on the phone. Fortunately, the event only occurred once a year so I didn't dwell on it. By the time my culture shock ended, I was interested in learning more about the kids who were trekking and what the experience was like for them. To date, I've not heard a negative report.

The notion of kids experiencing, albeit to a lesser degree, the hardships of those who paved the way for all of us, is a great idea. I'm unable to reenact my great-great-grandmother's trek from France to the United States in the bowels of a ship when she was 18 years old because I get motion sick. I have a doctor's note.

Although the handcart trek doesn't occur on Pioneer Day, the activity and resulting discussions were a smooth segue into the bonus July 24th holiday. Any excuse for a backyard barbecue and a parade is genius in my opinion. When I learned about Pioneer Day, I didn't fully understand what people were celebrating. But the holiday was legitimized for me when my husband had a paid day off. I did not experience culture shock adjusting to Pioneer Day.

Department and grocery store sales, special pricing on summer mountain sports activities like zip lines and alpine slides, all occur leading up to and on Pioneer Day. And the best part is a lot of people leave town because apparently this is the preferred time to have giant family reunions in the sticks. We're able to enjoy the festivities, yet ironically we don't feel the pressure of crowds and stress that accompany many other holidays. Every state should recognize Pioneer Day. The Mormons leave town, and the rest of us can celebrate that they came to town in the first place.

'Tis The Season

The doorbell rang for at least the sixth time that evening. My parents were visiting from Arizona for our first Christmas in Utah.

"Is that another goodie?" asked Dad as I returned to the kitchen with an object in my hand.

"It's an extension cord with a little rhyme on the note. They're 'extending' their wishes for the merriest of Christmases to us. That is so creative."

"An extension cord? Are you kidding me? I've never seen so much stuff. All those treats and odd items." Dad motioned to the pantry shelf that was the placeholder for the neighbor gifts. "Do you know all these people?"

"Not really. But they're so nice. My friend in Salt Lake City said when she first moved here, she wasn't prepared for neighbor gifts either. She said now she has all of her gifts ready in a basket so she can pass them out when people come to her door. Kind of like Halloween. I had no idea how many people do this until a couple of days ago. It's so fun!"

The doorbell rang again.

Dad said, "Quick. Run get a jar of Vicks and put a bow on it."

○●○

In neighborhoods outside of Utah, neighbor gifts are different. People might spread cheer via a plate of cookies, a bottle of bubbly, or some holiday candies. But the recipient list is much shorter. A handful—maximum two handfuls—of houses receives a special home-baked treat or small Christmas or Hanukkah themed gift. Holiday cheer, beyond a wave and shouting merry wishes, is generally only exchanged with the most intimate of neighbors. And even then, it's considered a special treat.

Now I'm spoiled and it's fun receiving the variety of gifts people so generously share. I'm also stressed-out every year as I try to think of a new, creative, affordable, not-too-time-consuming-to-make, neighbor gift for 40 people.

One year when ward boundaries changed, I felt compelled to give gifts to families in two wards, Chris and the boys delivered over 70 bags of jellybeans. No creative rhyme, no color-coordinated jellybean theme, just multi-colored candy in a triangle-shaped cellophane bag that looked like a carrot.

My neighbors, friends and I have discussed this at length. We all agree that none of us should feel any additional pressure around the holidays. If we have the time, energy and feel inspired to produce and share neighbor gifts, then we will. If it doesn't happen, none of us should worry or feel badly because no one expects a thing. We all understand.

Except, I'm the only person who's chosen to take a pass on the sharing of neighbor gifts. Like when your friends tell you they're wearing jeans to the party, but they show up all spiffy. Never fails. One of my friends will loudly bemoan neighbor gifts, "This year I just can't do it. We're simplifying in our house, you know, focusing on the Savior." Then on Christmas Eve, the doorbell rings and there stands one of her children with a gift. I see my friend in the front seat of her car, wearing lipstick and looking glitzy, passenger door thrown open with a box of dozens more doo-dahs to be delivered. I thank the child, wave to my friend while smiling, shaking my head and mouthing *You're too much!* Then I shut the door and call her a bad name under my breath for reneging.

This year I will give a pack of gum as a neighbor gift. Because I like gum.

Power Parties

"What'd you kids do this weekend?" Dad asked on our weekly father-daughter phone call.

"Not much. Puttered around the yard with the boys. Oh, and we went to a neighbor's house on Saturday for game night."

"Mormons play games?"

"Yesss."

"But they don't drink?"

"No. Definitely no alcohol, but it was fun."

And we did have fun. Game nights, potlucks and picnics are enjoyable. Quasi-dinner parties are a treat and Ladies' Bunco is awesome. The pacing of some (not all) social gatherings has required us to adjust. The tempo is speedy; and a Chinese fire drill, it is not. My husband has dubbed this type of party, the Power Party.

Mormon Power Parties are executed with precision, accuracy and attention to time. Specifically, the "Wrap it up!" time. People work together to set up tables, serve food, break tables down, remove garbage, clean dishes, put them away, all while engaging in light conversation. Before you know it, you've eaten a meal, had dessert, visited with "what's her bucket" and "what's his face" and are home wondering if the night was all a dream. A good dream, but did it really happen?

Compliments To The Party Planners—Seriously

Having had fun (again) with a few personal observations, I would like to share a cultural compliment. Segregation within ward boundaries does not occur. A person's age, occupation, bank account, personal style and sense of humor (or lack thereof) are irrelevant at a large social gathering. Everyone treats each other with equitable interest and mutual respect. Not that smaller sidebars don't occur among the special interest groups; mountain bikers, scrapbookers, old people. But for the most part, there's a feeling of acceptance. Cool people help the quirky people find the beat, and the quirky people help everyone else lighten-up.

There is an extraordinary amount of diversity (besides the fact that everyone's Mormon) at the social functions we've attended in our community. I like that.

Confessions

Mrs. and Mrs. and Mrs. Nelson

Polygamy fascinates me. I know that the LDS Church no longer practices plural marriage and people who choose to practice polygamy lose their Church membership. Most nonmembers understand this fact, although unfortunately there are probably a few people who remain confused.

A friend showed me the location of a well-known polygamist family home. I drove by at every opportunity hoping to get a nosy glimpse of the women and children. A few times women, children and a MAN were mulling about the property. They looked surprisingly normal. Not at all like the flowered-dress wearing, backcombed-bang sporting women we all see in the media. I considered placing

Bunco invitations—hosted at my house—in their mailbox, addressed to Mrs. Nelson, Mrs. Nelson, Mrs. Nelson and of course, Mrs. Nelson. If only I could chat with these women and understand why they would desire such a lifestyle, even if they believed it was righteous.

Clearly, I'm not the only person fascinated by plural marriage rooted in religion. TLC's recent reality show "Sister Wives" has been a huge hit. As a person with many LDS friends, I feel the show could do a better job of delineating LDS from FLDS. My fear is that for those people who remain perplexed by Mormonism due to ignorance, a show like "Sister Wives" might create more confusion and misperceptions. Confusion and misperceptions that the Church has come a long way in way righting.

Having said that, when my husband tells me one of his coworkers is a polygamist descendant (I recognize many Mormons are polygamist descendants from a generation or two removed, but I'm talking about people whose parents currently practice polygamy) and is *willing* to tell me what Thanksgiving is like at their house, I'm all ears. Talk to me.

We're All Dumb And Dumber

It's true that some of my nonmember friends and acquaintances are ridiculously ignorant about the Mormon Church. Friends who are educated, intelligent and broad-minded don't grasp the basic beliefs of the Church. Which is funny to me because people generally understand Judaism, Catholicism, Hinduism, Buddhism and Islamism. Well, maybe Islamism isn't consistently understood, but the argument that Mormonism is a new religion is ceasing to be an excuse for not understanding the basics.

We were visiting family in Colorado shortly after we'd moved to Utah. While having coffee with a few girlfriends one morning, they asked me if I still ran. (Running has been my Prozac for years.) I explained that the hills, beautiful scenery (mountains, meadows, quaint farms), trails, and bedroom community made for some of the best runs I'd ever been on. I also mentioned that I had found a few gals to run with.

"How did you find people to run with?" asked one friend.

"My neighbors. There are a lot of women who run."

"Are they Mormon?"

"Yes. Remember, unless I tell you differently, everyone I know in Utah is Mormon."

My friends looked at each other surprised, and then one of them asked, "Do Mormons run?"

I was stunned. "Well, yeah. They're not Amish."

My friends weren't unkind, they simply had limited exposure in their lifetimes to LDS people, and had no reason to learn about or understand the Faith. Their knowledge was likely limited to things they'd seen on the news over the past 50 years. And unfortunately, many of the topics that were media worthy in the last half-century didn't lay a fair or solid foundation for people to build upon. But I counseled my friends, and they are crystal clear on the fact that Mormons do indeed run. And they spit, and they get mad at their kids, and have troubles with their marriages, and not everyone bakes a good loaf of bread.

○●○

A friend was visiting from another state a few years ago. I took her to Temple Square, a common tourist attraction regardless of a person's belief system. She told me she was worried she might get converted. I didn't know what she meant. After chatting for a while, it became clear that she thought it was possible she could be the victim of some sort of hypnotic mind-control or mystical coercive persuasion. She was afraid to read the *Book Of Mormon* for fear of falling under its spell.

I love this friend, and she was able to laugh at herself by the end of her visit. But the point is honest; there are still people who view Mormonism as a cult-like religion. I'm sorry.

Check The Box On Adult Beverages

I've lived in my community for several years now. I still can't bring myself to purchase coffee at the local grocery store. I know it's my right and choice to buy and drink coffee, but it's like being at Olson's Mercantile from "Little House On The Prairie." People pay attention to the purchases of regular customers, especially when you're the only regular customer who isn't LDS. Mormon children stare at a giant coffee can in someone's cart. It's not comfortable. So I buy my coffee in bulk other places.

The word "coffee" feels like the word "sex" around here. As my friends and I discuss our morning pre-run rituals—one gal has a banana before our run, another a piece of peanut butter toast—my contribution to the conversation is that I enjoy a "hot beverage." If the use of semantics worked for President Bill Clinton, it might work for me. Unnecessary, I know.

Out of respect for the values in our area, I discreetly consume wine and bark at my husband if I see him in the backyard with an unconcealed beer bottle. Like the coffee, I recognize it is well within my husband's and my rights to purchase and responsibly consume alcohol. There are very few *close* LDS friends who I am comfortable drinking a glass of wine in front of. And it's not their issue; it's mine.

They're Still Curious

Many people want to know what it's like living in Utah with "a bunch of Mormons." Riding the ski lifts every winter, I'm asked multiple times by chair-mates from other states about my experience, *after* they've established that I'm not Mormon. Not much ground can be covered on a high-speed chair lift, but I've been a fair ambassador for the state and culture. I acknowledge that living in Utah isn't for everyone. The only demographic I've heard struggle are the nonmember divorced folks in their 30s and 40s who are looking to seriously date, possibly remarry, but aren't interested in an LDS single person. Singles wards don't appeal to a mid-life-y, divorced parent who isn't Mormon.

Questions about state run liquor stores, the accessibility of Starbucks, and frequency of Missionary visits are all common. Occasionally someone shares a "friend of a friend" story about a negative experience that allegedly occurred with Utah Mormons. Someone was shunned, a teenager converted unbeknownst to their parents, and Mormons only socialize with other Mormons. There might be a grain of truth in some of the stories. And I'm sure a person's bias also colors the tale. We're all just people. I assure visitors that I've never had a problem obtaining coffee, tea or wine, I have LDS *real* friends, and that our Mormon neighbors are kind and fall within the broad definition of "normal human being," except for that one man who never waves and won't eat foods that begin with the letter "K". But all neighborhoods have one of those.

The Cross

The cross is no longer only a symbol of Christianity. People wear crosses as jewelry and use them as home décor regardless of religious beliefs, so it's not safe to assume that someone displaying a cross is doing so to express their Christianity. However, I believe there are people in Utah who wear a cross not just to say, "I'm a Christian," but to say as loudly if not louder, "I'm not Mormon." I say this because I was one of those people.

At the height of my culture shock, when I felt lonely and angry and was tired of posing, I frequently wore a visible cross. There's nothing wrong with wearing cross jewelry, and I still occasionally do. But there was a time when it was important for me to identify myself as a nonmember, and that did the trick.

If I wear a cross now, it's because the turquoise goes with my outfit, or it was a gift from my mother (who, not that it's anyone's business, is so *not* religious).

Penance Probably Not Required

Titling this chapter "Confessions" implies that I've sinned. Perhaps we should refer to it as the Mormon Coffee Talk section. We're speaking freely, but not into the microphone. Like when Tic Tacs that have fallen to the bottom of a person's handbag or briefcase are publicly discarded, but privately enjoyed. Nothing terrible, you just don't want someone to see you eat a lint-covered Tic Tac.

Tough Love Observations

Although Mayberry overall is a shiny, happy place, there are some cultural issues worthy of discussion and an honest critique. I believe these issues are endemic not just to Mayberry or Mormonism, but also to certain socio-economic groups, and women. I understand the struggles surrounding competitiveness, intimacy and sexism. I've lost my footing on those slippery slopes many times. But the volume seems to spike on these issues in this sub-culture. It's sad for me to watch lovely people experience the unnecessary heartache and loneliness that accompany buying into unrealistic goals or ideals.

Competitive Nature—Kids And Parenting

There's a palpable level of competition among kids and women. I don't hang out with the neighborhood men, but it's *possible* the desire to win exists within their group, too. This is purely a cultural observation. We're all proud of our children and want them to experience conventional success. With thinly veiled envy, mothers congratulate one another on the academic, athletic or musical success of a child. Like somehow, the attractive, smart kid next door is an indication of one person's outstanding parenting, and another person's poor parenting.

Kids reek of the win/lose philosophy as they look at each other, summing up the field. Cliques exist everywhere, but the clothes, the lessons, the sports, the performances, and oh-good-heavens the hair, create visible social boundaries. It's like watching a race where the finish line is the edge of a cliff. There's no shame in attractiveness or academic, athletic, musical... *any* success. But I'm concerned about the value we—I abjectly include myself—place on these things. There's no doubt in my mind that the kids feel some of that misplaced value.

I've also heard mothers defend their child's rude behavior, express disbelief in a teacher's assessment of a situation, and refuse to see that the children they love so dearly, might be self-centered, at times unkind, and *possibly* unpleasant little people to be around. It's a shame.

Competitive culture and focus on achievement is nothing new in the United States, so it's not entirely surprising to witness the trend in this sub-culture. However, the occurrences of neighborhood bullying and insensitive teenagers have surprised me. I expected LDS kids who wear CTR rings to show each other more compassion and grace. I also expected their parents to model this behavior. Ouch.

I've listened to more than one person bemoan a socially ugly situation their child was involved in. I've listened to recounts of the blow-by-blow between the parents who are allegedly trying to help the younger people resolve the problem and hurt. And more than once, I've shaken my head and said, "*What* is CTR about that? About any of it?"

Utah County is not the only place with a community of competitive kids, it just happens to be the view from my window.

Competitive Nature—Women

Which brings me to the women. The supportive framework for women the Church offers and encourages is wonderful. The majority of women seem to sincerely desire to be a good neighbor, to serve and to do the "right" thing. There are also a lot of women who want to be the prettiest, fittest, tidiest housekeeper, best gardener, calmest speaking mother and finest culinary artist. (And, good luck getting that recipe.) All of this is *only* after she has displayed that she's in the running for the most righteous. Again, thinly veiled envy is unmistakable as the compliments ladies exchange pepper a social gathering.

Obviously not all kids and women fit my description. There are many lovely, humble and unpretentious people in my Mayberry sphere. Candidly though, I must report that the competitive set is significant.

Intimacy Issues

Intimate friendships have taken longer than is typical to establish here. I sometimes think women confuse venting and processing a personal problem, with gossiping. I finally have a few friends that I feel safe with and I believe feel safe with me. We all have issues, and sharing with a confidant or two can be cathartic. I feel like I've had to turn myself inside out, twice, in order to have someone feel like they can let their hair down with me. Be a girl. Laugh, cry, swear if need be. Then we can tell each other, "I've felt that, too. You're normal. Now blow your nose and get back in the game. You can do it!"

I recognize genuine friendships exist, but I've wondered if it's because I'm not LDS that it's taken longer for a woman to feel safe with and close to me. Had I implemented the Become-A-Jack-Mormon plan, maybe I would have been deemed close-friend worthy. I don't know. Perhaps other women in my neighborhood have felt as lonely as I have at times. The fact is that I've never had as difficult of a time growing and nourishing intimate relationships.

Who Wears The Pants?

When we first moved into our home, I felt a vein of sexism fed by a capillary of chauvinism running through the community. I don't feel it as much anymore, but it's still more prevalent than other places we've lived. For the most part, the chauvinism around here is more like the variety found in the

1930s "Our Gang" He-Man Woman Hater's Club; kind of silly and harmless. But my concern was that several of the husbands in the area wouldn't want their wives fraternizing with the new girl.

It wasn't just the stereotypical Utah County family model I noticed—Dad goes to work; Mom stays home, cooks, cleans, shuttles kids around, works on her son's Scout projects and smiles all the time because every day is a good hair day in Utah. There were strong patriarchal families. Young ones. Some families *appear* to adhere to a patriarchal model, but closer inspection often reveals a more balanced power distribution. I was surprised to find this wasn't always the case. To be fair, the situations I observed didn't look to have any unwilling female participants. Women weren't oppressed, per se, but seemed content conforming to a general definition of sexism.

My husband and I have assumed traditional roles in our marriage, but the power is evenly distributed. Usually.

Although I drink coffee and wine, and have a couple of teeny-tiny skeletons in my closet, I'm basically old-fashioned, have been married over twenty years and am hopelessly devoted to family. I couldn't be a better or more loyal sidekick in a friendship. But there were times I finally wooed a gal to be my friend, then after meeting her husband, her interest in our rapport appeared to wane.

This observation probably falls under "vision clouded by paranoia," but I did feel a few men were not excited about their wives becoming too close to me.

The Take-Away

We all grapple with the human condition. Every group of people shares the same proportions of human greatness and darkness. While I've called out competitiveness, intimacy, and sexism as endemic or cultural issues, I believe the issues exist for those in our community not because they are Mormon, but because they are human.

As a recipient of *real* tough love in my life, I choose to remember the important part, is love.

Mormon Myths & Nonmember Pitfalls

The nonmember grapevine is alive and well in Utah. People continue to perpetuate myths and instill paranoia in the minds of newcomers due to their own ignorance. We listened intently anytime someone offered advice or shared juicy nuggets of insider Mormon ploys, plots and odd behaviors.

Some pieces of information didn't pass the sniff test. For example, someone—a nonmember—told us the reason Mormons don't swim on Sunday is because they believe Satan is in the water. Upon first hearing this, I reacted like anyone would. Ew. That is *so* off.

The information *was* off, like other twisted and misunderstood facts people shared with us in an effort to be—I don't know—helpful. A grain of truth existed in a handful of stories, but comparing the original grain with the current myth is a classic illustration of the Telephone Game. One person whispers a story to another, and after several people have forwarded the tale, the final account is laughable.

However, a few of the cautionary tales we heard took us for a ride.

The CIA-Type File

Chris and I walked to the park with our kids on a sunny, Saturday afternoon. We were attending our first church social activity, a picnic. Everyone was gregarious, welcoming and appeared happy we had accepted the invitation.

We knew a few couples from the neighborhood, or we wouldn't have gone to the barbecue. We expected to chat with the folks we knew, make some new introductions, mingle, eat and head home. Just like any other social gathering.

We felt like the bride and groom at a wedding, struggling to make conversation with the friends of our parents. The friends who know everything about us, but who we know nothing about. People knew our names, the ages of our kids, which child had which medical condition, where Chris worked, and what we did for fun. Almost every person made it a point to greet us, and shake hands, sometimes forming a small line in front of us.

"That was strange," Chris said to me on our way home.

"We were the stars," I said.

"How did those guys know where I worked?"

"I bet they all read our file. They probably have to do their homework. A few of those guys were ready to go home but they hadn't met us, so they shot over to shake your hand. Felt like a receiving line."

"I wonder what else they know about us," Chris said. "I don't like it."

"I told you there was a file."

○●○

In hindsight, we were probably the first nonmember family to have attended a Church function in a long time. I'm sure word traveled quickly at the gathering when fresh faces appeared. People were happy to meet us, perhaps a little curious, and had good intentions. But, the over-the-top friendliness perpetuated the CIA-Type File myth.

In the event you don't know what I'm referring to (although I'm told a few LDS folks are still trying to get to the bottom of this conspiracy theory), rumor had/has it that there is a super secret file on every person or family within a ward. Exciting factoid if true. Does the file follow the person forever from ward to ward? Is the information electronically maintained? Is it on microfiche?

I've heard from a reliable source that there is no ward file containing personal information about my husband, our family or myself. I'm pretty sure only Santa Claus has that.

The Point System

"They get points for everything," a nonmember acquaintance said. "Even their failed conversion attempts."

"Makes sense," I nodded. "That's why they keep trying."

"The more points they have, the nicer house they get in Heaven."

"Does God keep track of the points?" I asked.

"Yes. And I think they report back to the Bishop so he can keep score on a scoreboard or report card."

Embarrassingly, I believed this myth for a while during my early paranoia phase. The persistent nature of a few people, after me saying, "No thank you," in English—the language all parties involved spoke—fueled the Point System myth.

A young woman who lived in a neighborhood basement apartment with her husband and new baby had the privilege of correcting the misinformation I had received. She and I were sitting on my family room floor playing with her baby.

"There's a Relief Society activity tonight. Interested?" the young woman asked.

"I know, but I think I'll pass. I'm tired." I was in full-blown paranoia. *They won't stop until I convert.*

We chatted some more, and then she mentioned something about her visiting teachers. I asked her a few questions, which I now know is a green light for many Mormons to "Go for it!"

She answered my questions then asked, "Would you be interested in a visiting teacher coming to your house?"

My cheeks felt hot, my heart pounded and I furrowed my brow as I said, "How many points do you get for asking me that?"

She laughed.

"Seriously," I said. "How many?"

Reliving the scene, I cringe and feel like an idiot. At the same time, someone's persistence, albeit filed under "well-intended righteous behavior," sustained the silly myth. That day marks my paranoia peak. I had a culture shock breakthrough as this sweet young mother convinced me that the Point System did not exist, nor were there sideline huddles of members discussing plays to "get" us with everyone shouting, "Break!" at the end.

This I know, if God has a whiteboard with tick marks behind all of our names representing righteous acts and general good-doobieness, I think we all might be surprised at the people who have the most points.

Shortcuts To Help A Novice Nonmember Newcomer (NNN)

Novice nonmember newcomers in Utah reveal themselves by their questions and beliefs in a few areas. There are several myths floating around, but I'll share five that should be filed under "Busted." If a member wants to help a NNN, clear up the following myths immediately.

1. *The Secret Handshake.* Either tell the person there is no secret handshake, or make something up quickly. They'll feel better if they're in the know. (And, yes. I'm aware of the temple endowment ceremony and understand there are rituals and symbols that are sacred. I don't believe that's what "The Secret Handshake" is referring to. Reputable sites like www.mormon.org and www.lds.org are wonderful resources for nonmembers…if they'll visit them.)

2. *Mormons Own The Pepsi-Cola And Coca-Cola Companies.* Men in particular are fascinated by myths surrounding Mormon businesses. Set people straight, and then refer them to Snopes.com because everybody trusts Snopes.

3. *Mormons Own Las Vegas, Casinos, and Brothels.* Men (business perspective) and some evangelical Church Lady-like women are all over this one. A simple, "Come on," as you chuckle and shake your head should cover it.

4. *Mormons Will Convert Your Kids.* Maybe we should all be honest here. If a NNN isn't rooted in their own religion or belief system and they haven't passed that on to their children, it is possible for a young person to be influenced by their Mormon peers and become a member. (Not that there's anything wrong with that.) However, the Church does not actively prey on children as potential converts, seizing every opportunity to proselytize when the parents aren't around. Let newcomers know they can relax. Their children do not have targets on their backs, but if parents are comfortable with their kids attending Church functions, members will happily bring them into the fold. Right?

5. *Mormons Can't Drink Caffeinated Sodas.* The confusion created for a virgin nonmember newcomer when they see members drinking Coke and Diet Coke, often first thing in the morning, is visible. The wheels of the nonmember's brain are heard clunking as they squint their eyes, head cocked, thinking almost audibly, "Hey. I didn't

think Mormons could do that." This one's simple.

Or is it?

Hopefully old myths will fade away, but new ones will certainly emerge. If there's anything I can do to minimize old or new myths, let me know. I expect both my file and the scoreboard to reflect my actions.

I Get Your Humor, Except When I'm The Joke

Details, Details

A brief conversation with some women at a Relief Society activity challenged my lifelong find-the-easiest-path to heaven or spiritual enlightenment plan.

"Look at Sue's eyes light up. She just saw me," I said to a couple of gals as I waved across the room to Sue. "She gets so excited when I show up at Church functions."

The women laughed.

"She's holding out for a conversion. I told her it wasn't likely, but she had my permission to baptize me when I die. I want to cover all my bases."

They knew I was spot-on about Sue and exchanged glances. One of the women said, "You know we can't baptize you for 100 years, though."

"You have to wait 100 years after I die?" I asked with concern in my voice.

The women nodded and looked suspiciously pleased with the level of concern I was trying to conceal.

"Someone make sure I get on the right list, then," I joked half-heartedly.

I went home and thought about this. What if Mormons are right and I die, where do I hang out for 100 years?

A week later, I was heading to the gym with a close friend. Her turn to drive, we exchanged hellos as I climbed in the passenger-side front seat of her car. My genius post-death baptism plan had a huge hole. I needed more information.

"Just out of curiosity—because you know, *I'm good*— when people reject the *Book Of Mormon* then die, where do they wait until someone can baptize them? Is it like a Mormon purgatory?"

"No. You get to work with missionaries," she explained.

"If you guys are right, I don't think I can handle missionaries for a hundred years," I said. "Sounds like purgatory to me."

"What? You can be baptized *one* year after you die."

"I was told I had to wait one *hundred* years."

"Who told you that?" my friend asked grinning.

My friend—the one who said I only had to wait one year—assured me she knew what she was talking about and suggested the other women might have been teasing. A few other people have added that there are rules requiring living relatives (children, not grandchildren—I specifically asked) to provide permission prior to baptizing the dead. But this is only for those nonmembers who are not related to current Church members. And I think there was something about a person's ability to recite the Preamble to the U.S. Constitution during their lifetime. Preamble reciters were moved to the top of the list.

I can't imagine Mormons yanking a nonmember's chain about something as important as baptism of the dead. But what's a girl to think? If everyone's in on the joke but me, then hardy-har-har.

For the official record, give me a day or two upon my demise and then hit me. I'll sign the required paperwork ahead of time.

Splitting Hairs

While working on this book, I shared earlier versions of chapters with fellow writing students in a local class I attended. In an effort to disarm LDS readers I went overboard in listing why I was qualified to write the book. The original introduction contained the sentence, "I've read several of the *Doctrine and Covenants*."

The LDS students burst into laughter, cackling and snorting. I didn't know what was so funny. Seemed to be a real knee-slapper though.

My teacher explained, "You mean you've read sections, not 'several' of the *Doctrine and Covenants*."

Probably an example of Writer/Mormon humor because it was a word choice issue that I venture to wager a few LDS people wouldn't have noticed.

Funny.

Famous Mormons—Fail

Once at a neighborhood game night, my husband and I reminded our friends that we are not familiar with all the people in the *Book Of Mormon*, nor did we attend BYU in the 80s. We have no idea who the quasi-famous student was who wore pink pants and strutted the campus, and the names of star athletes and coaches fly over our heads. If we were all going to play "Guess Who This Famous Person Is," we needed to pick more mainstream celebrities. Chris and I still lost. Game night is serious business around here, and the couples are ruthless.

○●○

The reality is, no one has ever made fun of us, teased maliciously, or tried to use humor in a hurtful way. I can even hang in some of the light-hearted Mormon dissing that my LDS friends sometimes engage in. I'm careful though.

When a friend's Gs are exposed, I might sidle over and whisper, "I see London, I see France…"

PART III

At The End Of The Day

Confidential To Nonmembers

(Who live in a predominantly LDS community.)

Most of Utah is more religiously diverse than where I live. But if you find yourself in a community where you are the only nonmember in your ward, have the tendency to jump to conclusions, are prone to the power of suggestion and/or have a propensity towards paranoia, allow me to help. You too can experience the joys (I'm serious and sincere) of life in a small Mormon town.

1. *Don't believe everything you hear.* This is crucial. People for the most part are well intended, but members and nonmembers alike are just *people* with their own histories, biases, baggage and perceptions. Your opinions—your story—must

come from your experiences. Build with an open mind and open heart.

2. *For some (not all) the bubble is real.* A few members have shared that they don't have close friends outside of the Church. The reason isn't because the person is intolerant; the reason is life hasn't presented the opportunity to commingle with many people who aren't LDS. There are members who have been born, raised, and continue to live in Utah County. An area populated mostly by Mormons. Recognize this, but don't assume someone's not interested in cultivating a friendship. Give them a chance.

3. *Give people and yourself multiple chances.* Bumping noses when you go in for a kiss shouldn't prevent future attempts. The payoff is always worth it. Be prepared for a few more head tilts, leaning in at the wrong time, pulling away too soon, but don't give up. I'm thankful people have afforded me the opportunity to clarify or rephrase my words as I've learned about Mormonism and my neighborhood's social norms. Patience in building

any relationship is important, but I've found it to be essential here.

4. *Accept where you live.* One of the reasons people live in our town, is because it's a Mormon community. Period. There is a lifestyle expectation that goes along with that. The religion is not the reason *we* chose our community, but serendipitously things have worked out for us. You will not change the fact that there isn't a market for drive-thru coffee shops, nor will you chase Mormons away by smoking cigarettes and drinking beer on your front porch. Although, you're free to do as you please. Your neighbors will likely smile and wave as they walk by.

5. *There's diversity, just look.* Make an effort to meet and get to know people. Everyone has a back-story, and I guarantee someone will be interested in yours. When the boldest tag I placed on someone was "LDS," I didn't allow myself to see the multi-faceted individual behind the label. As a self-proclaimed open-minded, non-judgmental, scoffs-at-stereotypes individual, my self-righteous values were tested. I became the antithesis of who

I *claimed* to be when viewing Mormons. Don't make the same mistake.

6. *Read the book.* You might find it helpful to understand the basic story. You might choose to convert, but if you don't you'll have bragging rights with your neighbors that you have *read* the material. I told an LDS acquaintance that I had read the *Book of Mormon* twice. She laughed and said, "That's two more times than most Mormons."

7. *If you have questions, ask.* I've joked that questions about the Faith are a green light for members to "Go for it!" Most members are forthcoming and happy to simply educate. A few times a person revealed her desire to proselytize, but more times than not, my questions were kindly answered. No strings attached.

8. *Lighten-up, Francis.* Don't be offended if someone gives you the *Book of Mormon* or attempts to proselytize. The effort will be gentle and sincere. You won't find people wearing sandwich boards with "Jesus Saves!" painted on them, pacing in front of your house while preaching through a bullhorn. The motivation behind mission work,

whether it's casual seed planting, or full-blown testimony bearing, is loving and sincere. It's easy to feel annoyed or angry, but know a person couldn't have truer intentions. No one has been harsh, rude or pushy to me in his or her proselytizing attempts. I felt offended, but what a waste of energy on my part.

9. *Never run or mow the lawn without a shirt.* You won't see a lot of skin in towns like Mayberry, even on a hot day. Spare yourself feeling naked. It's awkward.

○●○

If you do *not* have a propensity towards paranoia, are broadminded, and a nonmember living among Mormons, you're going to do great. Enjoy your pleasant neighborhood, the predictable rhythm of the community, and know that if you need anything, neighbors will *race* each other in an effort to help you.

Confidential To Members

(Who live in a predominantly LDS community. Like 98%.)

I hope it's fair to say, that one of the reasons you live in a Mayberry-like town (as described in this book) is because you want to live in a Mormon community. Compared to the LDS experience in other areas where a family has to drive far for seminary or church, and are in the cultural minority, I understand this in total. I also appreciate the desire to keep the community as culturally true to the modern-day Mormon experience as possible. This doesn't mean, "No nonmembers allowed!" but like any community with social norms, radical changes in demographics probably aren't welcome.

However, when a nonmember who plays well with others (hopefully how our family can be categorized) enters the community, there are ways to minimize a potentially clumsy beginning. Following are some feelings and thoughts you might find helpful, or amusing.

We're Not All Catholic

We have a cross hanging in our foyer. It's more of an art piece than a religious statement. Countless people have entered our home, commented on its beauty and asked, "Are you Catholic?" We're not.

Not being Catholic is hitch number one, but when I use the word "nondenominational" I can usually count on watching someone get wrapped around the axle.

○●○

I didn't have time to invite the missionaries in that day, and was disappointed to see new faces again. The prior pair had been sweet. Of the new pair, one young man seemed a little sharper than his companion.

After establishing that we were already familiar with the gospel and that we were not Catholic, the simpler companion asked smiling, "What religion are you?"

"We're nondenominational Christians," I answered.

"Oh. I met one of those once," he said bobbing his head vigorously, while the color drained from his sharper companion's face.

○●○

I generally avoid religious discussions, but there seems to be confusion surrounding the words "nondenominational," "agnostic," "evangelical," and "atheist." If you need clarification reference a dictionary. I have. Understanding the terms prevents all of us from inadvertently making the wrong assumption about someone's belief system. This is particularly important during the "getting to know you" phase of the relationship.

Use Of The Word "We"

"Thank you for everything," I said to one of the women at my 40th birthday celebration.

"We *all* just love you, Chris," she said.

"We" has been used many times by neighbors and acquaintances when the individual and I were the only two people engaged in a conversation. I want to say, "But what do *you* think about me, my family, our time together, etc.?" Phrasing comments with "we" adds to the perception of "us and them." This is our neighborhood, home and community, too. I feel another row of bricks being added to the wall that stands between loneliness and meaningful friendships when the suggestion is that we're guests.

When someone says "We *all* just love, care for, admire, etc., you or your family," the compliment is sincere. But the implication is that the person is a mouthpiece for *something*—the neighborhood, community or Church—and the unintended result is a reminder that we're outsiders.

Elusive Nonmembers

There must be other nonmembers in our area. I can't find them and there have been times I've suspected that members deliberately throw us off each other's scents.

"A family over there," my friend casually waves her hand in a southwesterly direction, "...are nonmembers. I think."

"Where?" I ask.

"That way," she points, but now it's northwesterly.

"Like a block or two? In our neighborhood?"

"Yeah. Somewhere over there."

Conversation over.

The feeling is awkward. I want to say, "Oh please, oh please, oh please help me connect with someone else who might understand a few of my feelings; maybe share a cup of coffee or tea."

In the same breath, the pink elephant we're both stroking as we speak makes me hold my tongue. My friend might feel like I can't be as close with Mormons, or that I want to form a "Mormon bashing" group. Or maybe there's a fear that if too many nonmembers connect, the vibe in the community will change.

Twice I've been given the telephone number of nonmembers in the area. One gal was actually a Mormon on sabbatical and was drinking beer before noon. Buh-bye. There wasn't a love connection with the other woman either.

As much as I'd like to connect with other nonmembers in Mayberry, it's not all about the alcohol and coffee. The social ritual is comfortable and I miss sharing coffee or a glass of wine with friends sometimes, but I don't need to get drunk on either beverage. There's a big difference. Just because two people are both nonmembers doesn't mean they'll have things in common and connect. The same is true for members, I know. But the nonmember dating pool is small and it would be tremendously helpful to know that my member friends are supportive of introducing me to others I might connect with. And not just the drunk people.

Let The Missionaries Do The Mission Work

Be a neighbor and a friend first and foremost. If it even smells like a person is trying to share their faith and belief system, the tone is set. Long-lasting friendships can be tainted by an early effort to proselytize. A new family in an LDS neighborhood does not want to feel like the first thing everyone wants to do is change who they are and what they believe. Especially when the new family might live there for many years.

My dearest friends couldn't be more different from one another. If I felt like my Hindu friend wanted me to be Hindu, or my atheist friend wanted me to abandon my belief in God, the relationships would dissolve. Friendships are a gift and I can't always explain exactly why I've bonded with someone, but the give and take—the lessons—are precious to me.

When my LDS friends blur the lines between Church outreach and our relationship, I sometimes feel confused and hurt. I'm one of the odd nonmembers who enjoy socializing with people through ward activities (because in towns like Mayberry, ward activities equal neighborhood activities). But I prefer Church outreach remain separate from my close friendships.

A person fulfilling their calling on behalf of the priesthood, bishopric, or Relief Society, by contacting my husband or me to extend an invitation to an activity feels okay. We've made it clear that we appreciate being included when appropriate. However, if we're informed off-the-cuff by a friend, we feel like an afterthought. Or the *She's only my friend because she thinks I'm close to converting*, feeling rises within me. I'm neurotic, but I hope my honesty is helpful in some way.

> NOTE: I caveat everything I've written in this section if a person has made it clear that they do not want to be included in future activities. My hunch is there are more nonmembers than not who close the door on attempts at pure *social* inclusion because they assume they're invited as

potential converts only. Sad and unnecessary for everyone involved.

Nonmembers expect missionaries to visit. Let the young men do their job. If there's hope, *then* help your new neighbor or friend learn more. It remains difficult after several years to separate early attempts to "help" me understand the teachings of Joseph Smith from the relationships I've developed with people. Even if the goal is righteous and one you believe in with all of your heart, it's better to hold your hand a little closer to your chest early in the game.

Clarify The Fun Part

Because neighbors and friends socialize primarily through ward activities, it *is* important to remember the nonmembers. If the activity is nonmember-friendly and the invitation is purely social, make that clear. I guarantee most people avoid going to functions associated with the ward because they think they're going to get the "talk."

Give a voice to the reality of the culture. Assure someone that it's the way block parties happen in Utah County. No one will pull them aside and work them (or their children) over. Church activities are a convenient way for neighbors and friends to visit and enjoy each other as people.

We all want to feel relaxed when we socialize, not braced for the impact. Your role as missionary members is fulfilled, in my humble opinion, by the simple act of including nonmember neighbors (without a catch) in the fun stuff. People like to have fun.

No Means No

And, "Maybe later, " means no, too. Ask any married person. In an effort to be polite, or simply not knowing what to say when caught off guard, a nonmember might avoid direct and mature communication. This leads everyone to think there's hope for a testimony bearing moment. Let it go. Especially when you're dealing with a neighbor and friend. Again, send in the missionaries if you believe in your deepest place that a person is seeking. Patience is rarely a bad thing.

Keep Your Shirt On

In the last chapter I told the nonmembers not to mow their grass or run without a shirt. A few times a Mormon neighbor-guy has done this very thing. We're trying to process a lot as nonmembers; please don't throw a wrench in the works.

Why It Works

Sometimes it's difficult to pinpoint precisely why a relationship or a situation works. If positive things result, why fight it?

I've candidly expressed to many nonmember friends that as happy as we are living where we live, they would likely be miserable. Photographs of the lovely setting where our neighborhood is nestled intrigue people. When friends and family visit, they always comment on the beauty and calm of our community. Occasionally, someone comments on the intangible cultural "feel" and expresses their discomfort and unease. I understand because I've felt the "different," too.

We've discussed relocating to a community 15-20 miles north, here in Utah, for several reasons. It's fair to say that religious diversity appeals to us but as more time passes, that diversity is less of an issue. We've also thought it would be nice to be closer to our sons' school, the places we shop, and my husband's office.

Every time we house hunt, we return home to Mayberry and can't bear the thought of leaving. Our sons share this feeling.

Possible Reasons For The Love Connection

1. *Our personalities.* I like to think that my husband and I are considerate, bright, aware and thoughtful people. We've made an effort. Our intentions are not to make waves at the expense of others, although we stand for what we believe in, hopefully with diplomacy, when necessary. We'd make good Mormons.

2. *We're able to escape the cliques.* Social drama occurs across the board for all people. The office, schools, bridge club, retirement communities, families, friends and neighborhoods all provide plenty of opportunity for cliques and social politicking. As a nonmember living among members, my social drama is greatly reduced. Because we live further

from our sons' private school, I've avoided much school related gossip (which occurs everywhere) and a variety of personal agendas.

3. *Our sons are friends.* Sometimes I worry that our boys don't socialize enough with kids outside of our family. The neighborhood kids are in established relationships and, like their parents, have full dance cards. We live too far from the school to arrange frequent play dates. Fortunately, our sons like each other. Except the little one. He has his crosshairs set on one of his brothers. Our boys also require more downtime than what appears to be the social norm, not just in our community, but everywhere. Fortuitously, our fringe position in the community minimizes social demands. Score another point for Mayberry.

4. *Insulation and predictability provide comfort to this family.* There's not much more I can say about this. Right or wrong, we're homebodies. My husband, sons and myself are comfortable with few surprises and feel safe in our cozy community, routine and schedule.

5. *It's possible I have a disorder.* I don't have agoraphobia because malls make me happy and I enjoy people. However, feelings of general social anxiety (something we all experience at times) might partially explain why the puzzle pieces snap together so well. The isolation we experience by not being an integral thread in the tightly woven community fabric could be a crutch, enabling me to remain in the comfort zone of my family room.

And finally…

6. *Divine design.* I'm open, if you are. It's a two-way street.

The Thank You Note

My mother used to tell me we only get mad at the people we love. "If I didn't care about you so much, I wouldn't bother to get angry or frustrated with you," she told me after a deserved scolding.

People, experiences, things, and places that affect us deeply often invoke mixed and powerful emotions. Life in Mayberry has contributed to feelings of loneliness, confusion, frustration, anger, and paranoia. But like yin and yang, there have also been overwhelming feelings of understanding, respect, friendship, safety, comfort, community, and gratitude.

Our children are being raised in a small, Utah County town. My oldest son has very little memory of homes prior. My other two sons know only Mayberry.

Within the first six months of moving into our home, one of our sons was diagnosed with type 1 diabetes and hospitalized for a week. Less than a month later, I was rushed to the hospital via ambulance due to complications with a miscarriage. It was a devastating time. A neighbor, who hardly knew us, brought food, respected our privacy and quietly and compassionately offered any assistance.

Women supported me when that third baby—the one I just had to have—arrived and didn't sleep for months. Frankly, the baby that is here due in great part to the encouragement from friends, "Girl, you're in Utah. You can be pushing your grandbaby in a stroller and nursing your own baby all at the same time. You're never too old!" They surrounded me as I turned 40, which wasn't long after having *that baby*. They have listened to me air my frustrations about *their* culture, complimented my tattoos when we've gone swimming together, and made me feel comfortable attending church related functions, or not attending.

My community is beautiful. For a girl born in the Midwest, I can't imagine life without the mountains that surround us. Utah is home. It's not just the stunning landscape in all directions that makes this place so wonderful. It's the people. The gracious, forgiving—more accepting and tolerant than I gave them credit for—sincere people. Most of whom happen to be Mormon.

With love, I thank you.

AUTHOR BIO

Chrisy Ross was born in Fort Wayne, Indiana, in 1966. Much of her childhood was spent in a small Midwestern town, catching crawdads and pretending she was Mary on *Little House on The Prairie* or Gypsy Rose Lee. She received her high school education in Texas during the 80s, prior to Ross Perot's heroic revival of the failing system. Her college world tour included University of Texas, Northern Arizona University, a few community colleges, and the University of Phoenix. Thankfully, she emerged able to read and write.

Chrisy currently lives in Utah with her husband and three sons. She's humbled by the surrounding mountains, enjoys skiing, running, the *idea* of camping, and spending time with her family and friends. Writing is a joy provided there is access to a thesaurus and grammar book.

To learn more, visit ChrisyRoss.com.

ARTIST BIO

Darrell Driver is proud to say that he's a self-taught artist. Creating through very late nights, determined to fulfill his passion for art, Darrell produces beautiful pieces that are rapidly gaining popularity.

He's constantly drawing and sketching, but Darrell recently fell in love with vibrant aerosol and oil paints. He found that if he incorporated the two, he could produce an unexpected and striking result. With no post-production in mind, Darrell begins a piece with a solid foundation of color and basic shapes, building from there. Inspired by everything around him—the people he meets, Utah culture, and his family—Darrell enjoys observing what keeps our surroundings in harmony.

Darrell hopes his art excites people and leaves them with a happy feeling. But he ultimately paints to get a reaction from his three children, and his wife, Amber. Her influence is the strongest in Darrell's pieces and, fortunately, she has a discerning eye.

To learn more and view the artist's work, please go to DarrellDriver.com or visit his Etsy shop at www.etsy.com/shop/driver1.